HALL OF FAITH SERIES

The Long Road to China

The Story of Dr. Harry Miller

JOY SWIFT

Pacific Press Publishing Association
Boise, Idaho
Oshawa, Ontario, Canada

My special thanks to Dr. Herbert Ford and Dr. Clarence Miller for their assistance in writing this book. Harry's life was truly an inspiration.

Edited by Marvin Moore
Designed by Tim Larson
Cover art by Jim Padgett
Typeset in 10/12 Century Schoolbook

Library of Congress Catalog Card Number: 90-62270

ISBN 0-8163-0960-4

90 91 92 93 94 • 5 4 3 2 1

Contents

Chapter 1
School Days

The sweet fragrance of fresh hay filled young Harry Miller's nostrils as he opened the doors of the dairy barn. Several of the cows mooed as the early morning sunlight pierced the opening. Grabbing a stool and a bucket from the corner, Harry sat down to milk the first cow. The ping of milk against metal softened as the bucket began to fill.

Harry had been thrilled to land this job at Mount Vernon Academy. With four children still at home, his parents told him he would have to earn his way through school as best he could. Having lived on a farm most of his life, he especially liked working with livestock.

Harry finished milking the first cow and moved to the next. When he was through he poured the contents of all the buckets into one large vat in the back of the pickup. The sweet milk sloshed out onto his overalls. Jumping into the cab, he slammed the door shut. The engine roared to life, and Harry headed in the direction of the campus kitchen.

"Well, Harry, you're early this morning," the matron called cheerfully as she kneaded dough for the day's bread.

"Yes, ma'am," Harry answered, dragging the heavy vat into the kitchen. "I've got a full day of studies."

"So tell me, Harry," the middle-aged woman inquired. "This being your last year here, what are your plans for the future?"

Harry shoved the vat into the refrigerator and leaned against the counter to catch his breath. "I've been giving it a lot of thought lately, and I think I want to be a doctor."

"An honorable profession." The matron's eyes lighted up. "Do you know that a new Adventist college is opening in Battle Creek next year? It will be called the American Medical Missionary College. Perhaps you would like to attend."

"I'll inquire about that," Harry said. "Now I must be getting ready for class."

Harry applied to the new school in Battle Creek and was accepted. That summer he sold religious books door-to-door to raise money for college. He didn't particularly like the work. He ate and slept in a different house every night. Sometimes, lacking any other place, he slept in a barn. But the experience taught him how to deal with people, and he realized how fulfilling service for others could be.

Harry looked forward to the beginning of the fall term. Being accepted in a medical school carried a certain amount of prestige. Student rivalry that first year bolstered the egos of many a young man, each one trying to impress the others with his past credentials. Harry was one of them. He learned the hard way that "pride goeth before . . . a fall" (Proverbs 16:18). His anatomy instructor called on him during class one day. "Mr. Miller, what is the epiphysis of the bone?"

Harry's knees trembled, and he glanced sideways at his classmates. He remembered reading the word but couldn't for the life of him remember what it meant. He gulped. "I don't believe I can answer that, sir."

"What, then, is the diaphysis?" the instructor asked.

Beads of sweat blistered Harry's forehead. The silence in the classroom felt suffocating, and he knew that every eye was looking at him. He felt two feet tall.

"That will do, Mr. Miller," the professor said at last. "You may take your seat."

The class continued, but Harry felt thoroughly disgraced. From then on he studied his books over and over again, practically memorizing each chapter in the lesson. He vowed never to be humiliated again.

Hitting the books was one thing. But the hands-on part of his education terrified Harry because he had an overwhelming fear of blood and death. He recalled the fireside tales his uncle told when he was a lad—horrid stories of strange happenings in the night. He knew they were only stories, but they had left a lasting impression on him that he could not erase. He hated graveyards, and as a child would run into the cornfield to escape the sight of a funeral procession.

Even in medical school, when a classmate died of pneumonia, Harry refused to attend the funeral. As his fear gripped him anew, he wondered if he would ever be a good physician.

Harry's money ran out before too long, so, like many of the students, he did odd jobs around the school and sanitarium to finance his education. However, freshmen rarely got the good jobs. Those were reserved for seniors.

Harry's roommate, Stoops, found a job helping a coroner with postmortem examinations, which didn't help Harry's problem at all. Postmortem exams were done to determine the cause of death or extent of disease. Doctors could learn a great deal about the nature of disease and thus help others in the future. Stoops gave Harry detailed accounts of how he cut open and sewed up the dead bodies. The stories made Harry's flesh crawl, and Stoops knew it. He ribbed Harry constantly, inviting him to help in the lab. But Harry always had an excuse.

One afternoon Stoops came home to report that an elderly lady had died in a fall and there would be a postmortem exam that night.

"Come on over and help," Stoops said excitedly.

"I have to study," Harry said lamely.

"You're a coward," Stoops sneered. "You're afraid to go."

Harry's fear of shame overcame his fear of death. He knew that if the guys found out they'd play all kinds of tricks on him, just to watch his hysterics. Suppose they put a kidney in his pocket or planted a whole cadaver in his bed! Harry would never live the embarrassment down. He *had* to overcome his unreasonable fear of death.

"Of course I'll go," he answered, mustering all his courage.

"Great!" Stoops said as headed for the door. "I'll see you there."

Harry's stomach clenched into knots the rest of the day, and he shuffled from place to place. He prayed that God would help him through this night. Why did postmortems always have to take place at night, when it was dark and spooky? He felt every passing moment, knowing that it drew him closer to a confrontation with every fear he carried within him. Would God really help him?

"Well, God only helps those who help themselves," he said out loud as the time drew near. "Perhaps I can just peek in and sort of test the waters. What if I faint right then and there?" He reached the building where the postmortem was to be done. Inside, he grasped the door handle and pulled it open. Light poured from the room, and his eyes blinked as he looked at his fellow students gathered around the corpse. Immediately, as if by a miracle, his fears melted, and a great calm fell over him.

From that night on, Harry was engrossed in anatomy. He grew so adept at it that his friends began whispering that he would be a professor someday. He applied for a job in the anatomy laboratory and was given a position that only months before would have been his worst nightmare.

In his senior year, Harry was made a student teacher in anatomy. It was a busy year for him as he contemplated his graduation and the beginning of his medical career.

Harry began to take an interest in a young lady in his class—Maude Thompson. Harry had never dated a girl before, and he knew that if he neglected his studies he risked failing his courses. He also realized that if he neglected his girlfriend, he risked losing her. So he took a great interest in seeing that she passed her courses. Much of their time together was spent with their noses in medical books.

Both Harry and Maude graduated from the American Medical Missionary College with the class of 1902. With diplomas and medical licenses secured, the two doctors were married.

Chapter 2
A Higher Calling

Dr. Oliver Tiding held a flashlight in one hand as he peered into Harry's throat. "Your tonsils have to come out," he announced. "They look awful."

Harry pulled himself into a sitting position. "Must it be done right away?" he asked.

"Come now, doctor," Dr. Tiding mused. "You've performed hundreds of tonsillectomies on kitchen tables for people all over Chicago. You know how simple it is. Surely you're not afraid."

"No," Harry sighed. "Just busy. I have so much work to do at the clinic. And I have several lectures coming up. How will I speak with a sore throat?"

"You'll heal fast enough," Dr. Tiding assured. "I'll use my new snare procedure, and those ugly old things will be out before you know it."

Dr. Miller braced himself as Dr. Tiding positioned the snare around the first tonsil and started to pull. Just then, the wire broke, sending Dr. Tiding sprawling and leaving Harry with an inflamed tonsil in a wire noose. The pain was excruciating.

Dr. Tiding recovered from his fall and reached into Harry's throat to grab the end of the snare with an instrument.

"There," he said, holding the tonsil up for Harry to see. "Sorry about that little mishap. I'm sure it won't happen again."

He was wrong. Again the wire snapped, and Dr. Tiding repeated the painful process.

"That's never happened before," Dr. Tiding apologized. He examined the broken snare. "You must have tough tonsils."

"Yes, well, I'm glad I only had two of them and not three," Harry croaked. He pulled himself from the table and stumbled out of the office.

Harry and Maude had been assigned to their first year of internship at the Chicago Clinic. Maude taught obstetrics and gynecology, while Harry served as resident physician and lectured on anatomy; dermatology; and eye, ear, nose, and throat instruction. He also assisted in teaching surgery at the missionary college. It was a very busy first year!

But now a new position was being presented to him.

"Dr. Miller," Stella Houser inquired one day between classes. "Have you considered what you will do in the future? With your medical career, I mean."

Miss Houser was a former secretary to the Foreign Mission Board of the Seventh-day Adventist Church. Although she was now a student where Dr. Miller taught, she was always on the lookout for potential missionaries.

"Oh, I don't know," the doctor answered thoughtfully. "I'm quite happy with my teaching and surgery here. Why do you ask?"

"I was just thinking how wonderful it would be if you and your wife could be medical missionaries in China."

Harry cocked his head. "China? Hmm. I once considered going to Mexico or Australia, but I never thought of China."

"Oh, there is a great need for missionaries there right now," Miss Houser said. "You and Mrs. Miller could do so much. Would you give it some thought?"

"I'll talk it over with Maude and see what she has to say," Harry replied.

That evening Harry presented the idea to Maude. Both were intrigued by the idea of being missionaries. The prospect of going to a foreign country seemed exotic and full of adventure. But they knew nothing about China, except for two cities, Shanghai and Peking, and they knew that the Chinese were excellent laundrymen. Maude had been quite satisfied with the work of the Chinese laundry downtown. If there was really a need in China . . . yes, this could be quite an adventure.

As the days wore on, Harry couldn't keep his mind off China. "What's the matter with you?" his friend, Dr. Arthur Selmon, asked him one day.

Harry explained his concern. "That's wonderful!" Arthur exclaimed. "You *must* go."

The next day Arthur pulled Harry aside. "I talked with Bertha last night," he said. "As soon as we're married, she wants to be a China missionary too. And she told me this morning that there are two nurses anxious to go as well."

When Stella Houser told the mission board that she had six people, all in the medical field, anxious to go to China, the board was elated. But they had no money to send them.

"The work is badly needed over in China," they told Harry and his friends, "but if you really want to go, you'll have to finance the trip yourselves."

The six young pioneers were crushed. "We can't even dream of coming up with enough money to finance such a venture," nurse Erickson cried.

"Do we all still want to go?" Arthur asked.

The answer was unanimous. "Yes, we do!"

"Then, God willing, we'll do it!"

And so they began to pray. They bought and borrowed books and studied China. They wrote letters to missionaries in China to find out all they could. They gathered together in the evenings to brainstorm. "We'll be going as more than medical missionaries," Harry said one evening, pacing the floor in front of the others. "We'll be spreading the gospel to the Chinese people. But where will we get Christian literature printed in the Chinese language?"

"We'll have to print it ourselves," Arthur replied. "We'll need a printing press."

Harry went in search of a printing press, but without success. And at every turn they learned just what an enormous task they were taking on. The Chinese alphabet consists of over 50,000 characters and would be very complicated to learn. They began to doubt if they would ever get to China.

A few offers for financial support trickled in, reassuring the group that their prayers were being answered. Then one day Harry got a lead on a printing press from the Barnhart and Spindler Company. He went to talk to the manager. "Sir, there are six of us who are trying to gather the necessary equipment and funds to be missionaries in China," he began.

The manager stared inattentively out of his office window, obviously far more interested in the pigeons on the window-sill.

"What do you want from me?" he asked tersely.

"We are in need of a printing press to spread the gospel to the Chinese people. We hoped you might have a small press you could donate to the cause."

The manager gave a sigh. "I'll have to see what I can do," he said. "Now if you'll excuse me, I do have work to do."

"Yes, certainly," Harry stammered. "Thank you for your time."

As Harry walked down the stairs and onto the street, he felt sure that he would never hear from Barnhart and Spindler again. But the next day the manager called him in.

"It looks like we do have a manually operated press we can donate, if that will suit your needs," the manager said, more cordially than the day before.

"Yes, sir!" Harry said, shaking the man's hand. "That's exactly what we need, because there will be no power to operate an electric one in China."

Harry hurried home, whistling a happy tune. He couldn't wait to tell the others.

Little by little, other items were collected for the trip. A relative donated a typewriter. The Mueller Instrument Company donated surgical instruments and an operating table. The Ohio and Iowa conferences offered to pay for their trip to China and give them a small allowance—about seven dollars a week for each of the Miller and Selmon couples—to see them through the first year. They were to pay the nurses out of this allowance. They were also given credentials to prove that they were in the ministry, and in late 1903, the little band was on its way.

Chapter 3
The Long Road to China

On October 3, 1903, the *Empress of India* left the pier at Vancouver, British Columbia, and moved into Puget Sound. Dr. Miller stood on deck with his companions, sucking in the fresh ocean air. Sea gulls soared overhead like vultures, alert to any tidbit a passenger or fisherman might toss overboard.

"I'm so excited," nurse Simpson giggled above the roar of the engines. "I've never sailed on a ship before."

"I don't believe any of us have," Bertha Selmon commented, holding her stomach and sticking out her tongue. Then she turned and laughed. "Let's hope none of us gets seasick."

"We're not going to get seasick," Harry said. "We're on our way, and we all feel fine." He squeezed Maude's hand, tossing a wink her way. "This is going to be like an ocean cruise—a great vacation before we get down to business."

As night fell across the sky, the missionaries retired to their bunks below. After a quick stop at Victoria, the ship headed out to sea.

Contrary to its name, the *Empress* was a small vessel, and the missionaries were given the cheapest rooms, one for the two men and another for the four women, right above the rumbling propeller shaft. The steady whine of the shaft kept time with the rocking ship until both grew monotonous.

"Harry," Arthur groaned from his bunk a few hours after they had put out to sea, "I'm beginning to feel sick."

"*You* feel sick," Harry moaned. "I feel absolutely green. I've never felt so sick in my life."

Arthur wrinkled his forehead. "Do you think we should check on the girls?"

"You go right ahead," Harry said, doubling over from the nausea. "I'm not leaving this bunk."

For four days Harry stayed in his bunk, unable to hold down any food. On the fifth day Maude persuaded him to go up on deck. "The fresh air and sunshine will do you good," she insisted. "Come on. I'll help you."

"All right," Harry sighed. "But my heart's not in this." Half-crawling and deathly pale, the young doctor made his way to the deck and collapsed. There he lay, sprawled across the rough wooden planking, gulping in the salty breeze. Finally he moved to a deck chair. Eight miserable days passed, and each minute felt like an hour to poor Harry. Not until they reached Yokohama, Japan, did he finally move from his chair. As he staggered down the ramp, too weak to carry his own baggage, he made a vow to Maude.

"I tell you, I'm going to stay in China for the rest of my life. I'll die before I go through another bout of seasickness like that. I don't care if I never see America again."

Little did he know just how many times he would cross that ocean by ship or plane in the decades to come!

Their first impression of the Orient was a bit shaky, for after thirteen days on the sea, all the streets seemed to rock under their feet. The streets were filled with rickshaws, whose owners were anxious to pull anyone around for a few cents. So the weary travelers climbed aboard a rickshaw and rode all over Yokohama and westward to Kobe. After spending the day visiting with a missionary couple, they returned to the port to catch the ship that would carry them on to China, but when they arrived they found that their ship had already left the pier and was far out in the harbor!

Quickly they hired a large rowboat, and the men rowed as fast as they could toward the ship. As they drew near, they yelled and waved their arms until a passenger saw them and a rope was lowered to allow them aboard.

In no hurry to repeat the miserable journey they had just endured, they all stayed on deck and leaned against the rail to watch the waves. To their relief, the seas here were calm. Before they knew it, Shanghai, the greatest city in the Orient, lay before them. Coolies—unskilled laborers—clamored at the docks for the privilege of carrying the few bags they had.

J. N. Anderson, the superintendent of the Seventh-day Baptist mission, escorted them to his headquarters. In this faraway land all missionaries were friendly toward one another, regardless of denomination.

Pastor Davis of the Baptist mission was translating the Bible into the Chinese language, and he showed them his work, painstakingly handwritten.

"So how do you say Seventh-day Adventist Church in Chinese?" Carrie Erickson asked.

Pastor Davis was happy to translate: *"Chi tuh fuh lin an hsi er hwe,"* which means, "Christ-Returning Sabbath Church."

"Well, at least it loses nothing important in the translation," Arthur mused.

After several days in Shanghai, the new missionaries prepared to travel west to Hankow—a five-day journey by steamer up the huge Yangtze River. Their final destination was a city called Hsintsai, deep in the interior.

The ship churned against the current, making frequent stops to take on cargo along the way. When they reached Hankow, the men were told that they must pay their respects to the consul general.

"I would advise you not to go into the interior," the consul warned. "It is no place for greenhorns."

"But that is what we have come to do," Harry and Arthur argued. "That is our mission."

"If you go to Hsintsai without knowing how to speak the language, you will probably never be heard from again. The people do not take kindly to foreigners."

Harry tipped his hat and stood to leave. "Thanks for the warning, but we'll be fine."

A missionary from Hsintsai who spoke Chinese, Erik Pilquist, met them in Hankow and offered to escort them into the interior. As he looked over the new prospects, he began to chuckle. "I'm afraid your American clothes won't do here," he informed them. "There are no laundrymen to take care of collars and narrow sleeves."

"No laundrymen!" Maude exclaimed in dismay. "I thought Chinese laundrymen would be everywhere."

"I guess we have no choice but to go shopping," Harry said.

"Hooray!" Carrie whooped. "I love to shop."

Harry and Arthur felt rather silly trying on the colorful ankle-length gowns, and they found it nearly impossible to find shoes. Their feet were too big. But it was even harder for the women because at the turn of the century, Chinese women bound their feet to keep them small.

As the awkward company stepped onto the street, they discovered that their easy American stride would have to be altered to accommodate the long, tight gowns. Harry felt as if he were in a gunnysack race as he struggled to keep up.

It was the custom in China for the men to wear a queue, or pigtail, as a symbol of submission to the Manchu government. By order of the empress dowager, all Chinese men were to shave their heads, leaving only a patch of hair in the back, which was then braided so it hung down in a queue. Often these were made longer with a pigtail wig. The men also wore a *mao-tze,* or skull cap.

"If we are to be accepted by the villagers," Harry told Arthur, "we should avoid being different whenever possible."

"I agree," Arthur said. "Let's get a haircut."

So the men had their heads shaved and bought pigtail wigs until they could grow their own. Arthur's light hair was hard to match, since everybody in China has jet black hair, but Harry was quite convincing in his new Chinese garb.

A bumpy eight-hour ride in a third-class Belgian railway train carried them 150 miles north to Sinyang. Erik Pilquist pointed out the window to a farmer plowing his field with water buffaloes and a crude wooden plow.

"It's like stepping back in time," Charlotte gasped.

"Yes." Erik nodded. "The Chinese don't value progress. They believe if these methods were good enough for their forefathers, they are fine today. They are fiercely traditional."

The train jerked to a halt in Sinyang, bringing an end to

still another stage of their journey. The pampered Americans gasped in horror as they entered the dirty, smoke-filled kitchen of the hotel.

A fire blazed on the dirty floor, and a single kettle hung above it, steaming with some strange, bubbling stew. The teary-eyed cook stepped back to wipe his sooty face with a towel, then used the same towel on the stirring spoon before turning once again to the pot. The Americans promptly lost their appetites.

Choking and sputtering, the missionaries stumbled upstairs to a large room divided into separate cubicles by straw partitions. The beds were bamboo racks with a wooden block for a pillow. In spite of their stomachs, the missionaries crawled into bed in desperate need of a good night's sleep.

But Americans were a rare sight in Sinyang, and the hotel owner wanted to honor his guests with a musical serenade that lasted well into the night. They finally managed to get a few hours of sleep, but they were awakened early the next morning by a ruckus outside. Erik Pilquist went outside to see what was happening, and he was instantly surrounded by coolies, each one begging to be hired to carry equipment and haul the wheelbarrows to Hsintsai. The Americans rose quickly, anxious to begin the last leg of their journey.

From here on, several soldiers with rifles accompanied them. As the caravan moved out of Sinyang, food vendors pressed in to boast their products, but everything was so filthy that the missionaries didn't eat a thing the entire first day. They traveled fourteen hours that day. The villagers watched them with much curiosity and whispering.

"What are they saying?" Carrie asked.

"They are calling us foreign devils and foreign dogs," Erik whispered. "A few years ago the Manchu empress dowager ordered all foreigners killed in opposition to Western encroachment on China. Many missionaries and thousands of Chinese Christians were slaughtered. After the massacre, the Western nations demanded that the mayor of each city be responsible for the lives of the foreigners. That's why the soldiers are accompanying us."

"Will they use their guns if the villagers try to harm us?" Charlotte asked.

"Most of the guns do not work," Erik said. "They are old American Civil War surplus rifles. But that doesn't matter. As long as they look like they work, the villagers will keep their distance."

That night their hotel consisted of one big room, with no privacy partitions. But the Americans were too exhausted to care. Doubts began to spring up in Harry's mind as he crawled into bed, his body aching from the long miles. Maybe they should have stayed in Hankow and started their medical missionary work there. Why had he and Arthur insisted on going far into the interior, where there would be no English-speaking people at all? Perhaps the consul general had been right after all.

In spite of all the dreams and efforts they had put into getting here, their hopes so high, the young doctor now realized what an enormous task lay ahead. Had he led his companions into a situation that was too great for them? Would the villagers allow them to stay? Would they ever accept foreigners?

Harry looked at Maude, who lay sleeping peacefully beside him. Had he done right by bringing her to this primitive, forsaken country? What hardships lay ahead for her? She deserved so much more.

For two more days the caravan trudged onward, stopping only briefly along the way to help the sick. They bought fried pretzels and boiled their water before drinking it. As the sun began to set on the third day, they sighted the gates of Hsintsai. Harry battled his conflicting emotions of relief, anticipation, and fear. After thirty-eight days of travel, the missionaries were finally home!

Chapter 4
The River Trip

Mrs. Pilquist rushed to meet her husband at the mission station in Hsintsai. Squeals of delight filled the air as two small children tumbled into their daddy's outstretched arms.

"My, my!" Erik exclaimed as he hugged them tightly. "You'd think I'd been gone for a year! Mama, welcome our guests while I try to calm these two monkeys down."

Mrs. Pilquist turned to meet the new missionaries. "I'm so happy you've come," she said, clasping her hands in delight. "I do hope your journey wasn't too tedious."

Harry laughed nervously. "I'm afraid it was a bit rougher than we had expected, but we have arrived safely."

Harry and his companions scanned the tiny village. The crude little huts squatting upon the land seemed humbled by the great forest standing tall and ominous against the sky. A young boy in ragged attire watched from behind a tree.

"Well," Mrs. Pilquist broke in happily, "I'm sure you're all anxious to see your new quarters. Let me show you to them, and you can wash up while I finish preparing supper. You must be famished after such a long journey!" Mrs. Pilquist led the Millers, the Selmons, and the two nurses to their new apartments. "Now, they are small," she warned. "But I have done my best to see that they are clean. I do hope you approve."

She opened the door to the first apartment and led the Millers inside. Harry and Maude surveyed the tiny room furnished with a table, a bed, a lamp, and little else.

Maude forced a smile. "This will do just fine." For the most part her fears were quieted.

"OK, then. If there's nothing you need, I'll show the others to their quarters," Mrs. Pilquist said, pulling the door shut. "Plan on supper in about an hour."

"Thank you," Harry called as the door closed. Then he turned and faced Maude. "Well," he said with a sigh, "are you disappointed?"

"Not really. A little surprised. I didn't think the interior would be this primitive, but I'm not disappointed."

"We have a big job ahead of us," Harry said soberly. "I hope we're up to it."

"With God's help, we'll do fine. Now let's get cleaned up." Maude poured water from a pitcher into a bowl. "This is *one* meal I do not intend to be late for!"

At supper, the newcomers learned just what foods they would be living on as they filled their plates with rice, noodles, peanuts, and a syrup made from malted wheat. Harry dipped a peanut into the syrup and popped it into his mouth. "Say, that's not bad," he exclaimed, smacking his lips. "Not bad at all."

"I'll say," Arthur commented, his mouth half-full of noodles. "It sure beats the food vendor's fare."

"Yes," Mrs. Pilquist agreed. "But we have very little variety here. You'll see when you go to the marketplace."

"So tell me," Harry inquired. "How would you suggest we go about learning the local language?"

Erik thought for a moment. "I think the best way would be to have someone tutor you. I know an old professor who would probably be interested. I'll introduce you tomorrow."

Unfortunately, the old professor could neither speak English nor teach very well. Still, each day the Americans obediently gathered in front of him as he stood beside a propped-up board, on which he had written over 200 strange squiggly characters—a weird assortment of asterisks and intersecting lines.

"*Li*," the wrinkled old man pronounced perfectly, pointing to one of the symbols.

"*Li*," the missionaries repeated in unison.

The stooped little man jabbered his praise and turned to introduce another strange symbol. Day after day, they imitated the sounds made by the professor.

"Harry," Maude asked one day as they finished the lesson. "I know we're making all the right sounds, and we know which symbols go with which sounds, but do you have any idea what in the world we're saying?"

Harry chuckled. "Not the slightest, but have you noticed that Carrie seems to be conversing with the village children? Perhaps we should ask her what her secret is."

"It's no secret," she told them at supper that evening. "While you have been wasting your time with that old man, I've spent my time at the marketplace. The children are more than willing to tell me the word for anything I point to."

She paused to fill her chopsticks with fluffy brown rice. "For instance, rice is pronounced *mi*. And this peanut is a *hua shun*. I may not know how to write it, but I've developed quite a vocabulary. You should spend more time at the marketplace."

From then on, the missionaries went to the marketplace every day, buying only enough food for that day. That way they learned far more than they ever would have learned with the tutor. Soon they were conversing adequately enough to be understood. The tiny village of Hsintsai was beginning to feel like home!

After several months, the Pilquist family moved to a town about twenty miles away, but by now, the new missionaries knew enough Chinese that they felt comfortable being left alone.

In the spring of 1904, Harry and Arthur made their first trip out of Hsintsai. They headed on foot to Sinyang. Once there, they boarded a train for Hankow, where they were to pick up provisions along with some freight that had arrived from America.

They decided to save time and money by renting a raft for the last part of their trip home. A navigable river ran from Sinyang back to Hsintsai, and it would be far easier traveling that way than bringing all their goods home by oxcart. As a bonus, they could sleep on the raft at night while the boatmen poled up the shallow river.

The boatmen lived in a small hut right on the raft. They even kept a patch of soil on the raft where they grew a small garden to sustain them on their journeys.

But the days passed slowly on the shallow river as the wooden raft, burdened with heavy supplies, fought against the rocky bottom. In many places the boatmen were forced to travel ahead on foot to dam up the river before they could continue.

"I think I'll take a helper and buy some charcoal in the next town," Harry said after several days on the slow-moving stream. "At the rate we're going, I should be able to meet you upstream with no problem."

"Good idea," Arthur commented. "It'll save time in the long run, and the women will be happier if we keep the apartments warm."

Harry and the helper walked all night, arriving at the charcoal market the next morning. Together they hauled the heavy bags down to the riverbank to await the raft. But it did not come. Soon word came from a messenger that the raft had been attacked by bandits in the night, and the men aboard were badly hurt. Alarmed, Harry and his helper hurried downstream. Several miles away they found the raft pulled up on the bank. Arthur's arm was badly injured, and the boatmen were covered with bloody gashes.

"What happened?" Harry asked, stooping to administer first aid to his friend.

"Apparently we were being watched when we cashed in our American checks for silver in Hankow," Arthur speculated. "I suspect they've been following us all along."

"So did they get anything?" Harry asked.

Arthur shook his head. "Surprisingly, no. They tried to climb aboard, but the boatmen jabbed them with their poles. I threw stove wood at them until they finally gave up and left."

"Well, I'm thankful you're all OK," Harry said. He finished

bandaging Arthur's arm and rushed to retrieve needle and thread with which to sew up the deeper gashes.

"You know what surprises me?" Harry asked. "The boatmen could have helped the bandits steal all of our supplies, but they remained loyal to us, the foreigners."

"Yeah," Arthur agreed. "It's a good thing they did, or I'd be dead right now."

Harry finished sewing up the wounds and then began to reload the supplies onto the raft. As he loaded, a messenger came with a letter from Erik Pilquist saying that his wife was very ill and asking one of the the doctors to come immediately.

"I'll have to go," Harry told Arthur. "You take care of that arm."

"We'll wait for you," Arthur called as Harry walked away. "If you aren't back within twenty-four hours, I'll assume Mrs. Pilquist needs more attention, and we'll go on ahead."

Dr. Miller and the messenger made their way by foot and pony back to the city where the Pilquists now lived. Mrs. Pilquist had suffered a gallbladder attack but was now doing much better. After tending to her needs, Dr. Miller excused himself and headed out alone to rejoin the raft.

Rain fell in great torrents, and the narrow paths turned into streams, making travel difficult. Harry hurried along, anxious to reach the raft before it left, but when he reached the appointed spot, the raft was not there. In despair, he threw himself down upon the bank.

He was tired and hungry and soaking wet when two soldiers came upon him and carried him off to the district magistrate, where he was questioned thoroughly. When the magistrate was convinced that Harry was only trying to catch up with his raft, he insisted that Harry rest up before going on his way.

Although the accommodations were generous, Harry felt uneasy. The room reeked with the smell of opium, and he knew all too well the effects of the drug. Opium addiction was quite an epidemic in China in the early 1900s. It was smoked much like marijuana is today, but it was highly addictive and often caused death.

Harry climbed into bed, his eyes and nostrils stinging from the harsh smoke. He pulled the quilt up over his face and drifted off to sleep. The next morning when he stepped outside, he found the magistrate's own sedan chair ready to transport him back to his raft. Four coolies bowed to lower the chair, and Harry climbed in. With a shout, the parade moved forward.

A horseman rode ahead carrying a large red umbrella above the doctor to tell everybody that here was a very important person. Four more coolies trotted along behind to relieve the first four when they grew tired.

Dr. Miller sat back and enjoyed the pampering, remembering the days when the villagers along the way called him the "foreign devil." And now he was being treated like royalty!

The parade trotted along at such a good pace that they caught up with the raft shortly after noon. Harry chuckled triumphantly as the bewildered Arthur welcomed him back on board. The rest of the trip was uneventful, and the two husbands were glad to reach home.

The women exclaimed with excitement as the men brought out gifts they had bought in Hankow and foods that could not be found locally. A special feast was served that evening, and they all gave thanks to God for bringing them safely back together. Harry hoped it would be a long while before another such journey was necessary.

The missionaries served one full year in Hsintsai until they could speak the language well enough to separate and form new missions on their own.

"It is time to be like seeds in the wind," Harry announced at their last supper together. "It is time to scatter and bring new life to areas not yet covered. May God bless our efforts."

Carrie Erickson and Charlotte Simpson remained in Hsintsai to further the work there, and the Selmons went to Hsiang Cheng a few miles north. Harry and Maude moved with the printing press to Shangtsai to be close to the railroad for convenience of shipping and supplies. They packed their bags onto an oxcart and headed on their way.

Chapter 5
Start the Presses!

Harry carefully unpacked the Franklin printing press from its crate and ran his fingers across the shiny metal, admiring the machine that would allow him to reach the people with the message of salvation. From another crate he retrieved a box containing a font of Chinese characters—nearly 3,000 in all—and placed it beside the press.

Opening the box, he sorted through the characters, searching for the ones that would spell, "The Gospel Herald"—the name he had chosen for his new tract. But he soon found that searching by hand for each character necessary to print even a one-page tract would take too much time.

"I'll have to build a rack," he said to himself. "It will need pigeonholes for each of the characters." He turned to study the room. "And I'll need some shelves and tables for work space." Pulling a pencil and paper from the crate, he began to sketch his plans for the furniture he would need.

Satisfied that he knew just what materials to buy, Harry set out for Hankow. A crowd of twenty or so Chinese men watched as the pine boards were loaded onto a railway car.

"That is very fine wood," one of the men said as he tested a plank for splinters. "Do you intend to build a coffin?"

"Oh, no," Harry answered politely, climbing atop the stack. "This wood is going to become tables and racks for my printing press."

"A pity." The man shook his head. "Such smooth boards would make a fine coffin."

Harry's helpers had warned him to keep a close eye on the lumber coming home, for it was a prime target of thieves. The Chinese head of the household always kept a polished pine coffin in his home. It was a prized possession, and it was considered good manners for visitors to compliment a man on his fine coffin. Harry was determined that this lumber would make it home to the printing press.

Harry spread out his bedroll on top of the pile; then taking his black medical bag in hand, he turned to step down from the railway car.

"Pardon me," Harry said, searching for a spot among the men to climb down, "but I must pay for my lumber before the train leaves." He jumped off the train and hurried over to the man who had supervised the loading. Moments later he returned to find his bedroll missing.

"Did you see someone take my bedroll?" he asked the men still leaning against the railway car.

"No, no!" They all shook their heads.

Harry climbed aboard once more. He searched the crowd below, hoping to spot someone with his bedroll, but even if he had spotted the thief, he could not have left the lumber to retrieve it.

Just then the engine snorted, and the train lurched forward. Seeing no one suspicious, Harry lay down and prepared for the long journey home without a blanket to keep him warm. He did not blame the one who had stolen it, for it was likely that the thief needed it worse than he. The poverty-stricken people saw no wrong in stealing as long as they were not caught. In their youth they were taught to take what they could. Many times Harry had witnessed a child snatch a bit of food in the marketplace. It didn't seem right to stop them when they were so hungry. But he was thankful to arrive home several days later with his lumber and his medical bag intact, for in it he carried all the money he had!

Dr. Miller and his helpers worked hard to build the tables and stands and racks. Once built, the Chinese helpers labeled the boxes and put the characters into the appropriate cubbyholes. They fashioned their own ink rollers and inkstand, and after a few experiments with the ink, which insisted on freezing in the unheated shop, the little printing press was in business.

Everyone gathered around as Harry ceremoniously rolled the first tiny tract off the press. His helpers listened intently as he read the wonderful news of salvation out loud. As the days at the press wore on, the helpers were very loyal to the work, and many taught themselves about Jesus through the printing of the single-page tract.

Harry knew that not everyone could afford to buy his little Christian tracts, nor could he afford to give them all away. It cost precious money to print them up, and they had so little to work with. So he gave them out when he sold medicine in the dispensary and charged only those that could afford to pay.

Harry did not realize just how many people he reached with the tiny tract until he watched one of his customers as he left the dispensary one day. The little man walked to the center of town, climbed onto a rock, and began to read the tract out loud. A crowd gathered before him, listening intently to every word. One of them parted from the crowd and came into the dispensary.

"I cannot read," he said, "but my son can. If I might have a tract too, my son will share it with my whole family."

Reading material was scarce and always caused a stir. So Harry sent colporteurs out to distribute the tracts throughout the villages.

For seventeen months the young missionary couple worked hand in hand through the roughest of hours and the smallest of victories. Just as they were beginning to see some fruit from their labors, Maude fell sick.

At first she insisted on continuing her daily chores at the house and dispensary, but gradually she weakened until she had to turn the work over to her helpers. Her body wasted away. The two nurses, Carrie Erickson and Charlotte Simpson, were called on to care for her. Finally the mysterious disease won, and on March 14, 1905, Maude Miller died at the age of twenty-five.

Arthur and Bertha Selmon came for the funeral. A gray cloud hovered over the missionaries as they laid Maude to rest in a polished pine coffin beside the tiny chapel that Harry and Maude had brought to life. Dr. Maude Miller was to be the first Seventh-day Adventist missionary to give her life in the service of China.

Harry bore his sorrow in silence, but everyone knew the tremendous burden he carried.

"Come home," his parents wrote. "You need to be with your family in your sorrow."

But Harry would not hear of it.

"I have a mission," he wrote back. "Now, more than ever, I am determined to stay and help the poverty- and disease-ridden people of China. More than ever, I want to offer them the hope of salvation."

For two years Harry worked alone at the press and dispensary. He buried himself in his work. His only respite each day was when he knelt beside Maude's grave and prayed that God would bless his work to compensate him in some small way for his loss.

Two years after Maude's death, Arthur and Eva Allum, newlyweds from Australia, were sent by the Foreign Mission Board to help Harry in his work. Harry was excited about their arrival. He tidied the apartment that he and Maude had shared and moved into a smaller sleeping room.

Arthur Allum worked with Harry at the dispensary, where he was quickly confronted with the problem of opium addiction. Day after day the addicts were carried in unconscious.

Arthur held a patient down while Harry inserted a tube into his throat to pump out his stomach.

"This is the same man we treated four days ago," Arthur said.

"I know. Just keep him awake," Harry muttered impatiently. "Maybe we can save him for the next time."

Arthur slapped the patient's face and shouted in his ears. "Wake up, man. We're trying to keep you alive!"

At last the immediate crisis was over.

"Do you ever feel like you're winning the battle but losing

the war?" Arthur asked, as he sterilized the stomach tube.

"Every day." Harry shook his head. "Every day."

Harry's parents continued to beg him to return to the United States, but he refused to go. Finally they sent his brother Esta to China along with a friend, Orvie Gibson. Esta was a loyal worker, and Harry was glad he had come.

Harry wanted most of all to teach the people how to help themselves, and this was the main purpose of the dispensary. He felt especially frustrated by the Chinese lack of cleanliness. They understood little about sanitation, and often a successful operation ended in death simply because the family failed to keep the wound clean. They actually feared that bathing would cause pneumonia and other diseases! Many were the patients who came to him with huge, pus-filled ulcers on their arms and legs. The local doctors would cover the wound with plaster, thus binding up the pus and causing a bigger sore. Harry's treatment was alternating hot and cold water baths to clean out the pus and promote circulation.

But the people refused to bathe. So Harry came up with a way to trick them into bathing. He added potassium permanganate to the hot water, which made it look red, and methylene blue to the cold water. The people were more than willing to administer the red and blue medicine. Harry's treatment became famous all over the countryside, and people came from miles around to receive his special cure. If they could only accept that simple sanitation was the cure!

As the work progressed, the need for a bigger facility closer to a central shipping and supply area became evident. But the funds were simply not available. Until now all the work had been accomplished with the missionaries' own meager salaries and savings! The average daily wage in China was equal to five American cents, so little help could be expected from the people. But with God, all things are possible, and Harry knew that somehow the funds would come.

When a Wisconsin man donated a thousand dollars to the cause, Harry was able to purchase a piece of land near the railway station in Sinyang and hire local craftsmen to begin construction on a new two-story stone building.

With the help from the Allums and Orvie, Harry and his brother carefully packed the medical supplies and press equipment into crates and labeled them in readiness for the move. But in Sinyang they could find no place to rent while they waited for the new building to be completed. Their only alternative was to move into one of a row of beggars' dens below the railway station.

Consisting of three mud walls with the fourth side open to the weather, the stench of the dens attracted hordes of mosquitos. Lizards crept along the walls. The missionaries stacked the crates into the den and settled in as best they could.

A short time later, while Orvie and Esta were in Shanghai, Harry came down with a terrible fever.

"What can we do for you?" Eva asked. "What could possibly be the cause?"

"My guess," Harry answered weakly, "is that I've contracted typhus from the lice in the den. Tell Arthur to get some quinine to bring down the fever."

Eva Allen called for her husband, but by the time he returned with the medicine, Harry had grown worse, and now lay unconscious.

"What are we going to do?" Eva cried, sponging Harry's forehead with cool water.

"I don't know," Arthur answered. "If he comes around, I'll take him to the hospital. That's all I know to do."

Arthur and Eva kept a constant vigil on Harry until at last he opened his eyes.

"You had us mighty worried," Arthur exclaimed. "Here, take this quinine. I'm taking you to the hospital."

Arthur gave Harry four times the normal dose of quinine to counteract the high fever. Then he lifted him up and carried him to the train.

While they were traveling, Harry's fever broke, and before they arrived at the hospital, he felt much better. But now Arthur had come down with the same high fever. Harry left the train to buy more quinine and quickly gave some to Arthur. By the time they arrived back in Sinyang, Arthur was feeling much better too.

But back at the den, where Eva had been left to guard their equipment, she lay feverish and half-conscious. A quick dose of quinine eventually brought her around. They learned later that they had all been stricken with malaria.

While they were still in the beggar's den awaiting the completion of the new building, a missionary family from Shangtsai came seeking Dr. Miller's aid. Mrs. Westrup's eyes crossed so badly that Harry was amazed she could see at all. They had heard about Dr. Miller's remarkable success with eye surgery and asked if he might operate. Harry was more than a little surprised.

"I'm sorry," he protested, "but all of my medical supplies are packed away. I don't have anywhere to operate, and I certainly can't perform such a delicate operation in a beggar's den. The place is crawling with lice and mosquitos!"

But the Westrups continued to plead with him. "We have prayed about it, and we know that you should do this. We have cast lots, and each time God has said you should operate."

Westerners often expected more than the Chinese. The risk of infection was just too great. But the Westrups persisted until finally Harry gave in.

The Allums dug through the crates in search of the necessary medical supplies while Esta and Orvie fashioned a tent from a couple of sheets and some bamboo poles to be used as an operating room. Dr. Miller sterilized the instruments over a charcoal fire, praying all the while for God to bless his efforts in spite of such adverse conditions.

Mrs. Westrup lay on a bench under the makeshift tent. While Mr. Westrup and his young son shooed away mosquitos, Eva assisted Dr. Miller in the delicate operation. Amazingly, the surgery was a success!

Chapter 6
Harry Takes a Wife

Harry leaned against the dirt wall of the beggar's den and turned the envelope over in his hands.

"Who's it from?" Esta asked.

"The Foreign Mission Board," Harry said. "I wonder what they want."

He slipped his finger under the flap and removed the letter.

"Dear Dr. Miller," he read aloud. "The board has decided that since you are unable to perform any meaningful tasks until the new building is complete in Sinyang, we are sending you back to America on furlough . . ."

Harry scanned the rest of the letter and stuffed it back into the envelope.

"Why are they sending me back and not the others?" he pondered. A lizard scurried across his legs and disappeared into a crack in the wall.

"I have an idea," Esta said suspiciously. "Every time Mom writes to me, she asks if you've found a lady friend. Dad has probably let her concerns be known to the Mission Board."

"I'm being sent back just so I can meet women?" Harry lamented.

"Don't be surprised." Esta slapped him on the back. "Mom will go to any length to take care of us kids."

Harry began to grow his hair back in advance so as not to cause undue attention in America. But it wasn't easy parting with the beautiful waist-length queue that had taken four years to grow!

Two weary months of travel finally brought him to St. John, New Brunswick, where his parents now lived.

"Oh, Harry!" his mother called as she rushed to meet him at the train station. She wrapped her arms around him and planted a kiss on his cheek. "I have so many plans. I have a special dinner planned for tonight, and I've invited a lovely young lady to join us. She reminds me a great deal of Maude."

"Mom, that sounds very nice," Harry said. He hugged her tightly. "But if you don't mind, I would like to retain my right to choose my own lady."

"Of course, dear," his mother said. "I'm just trying to help. If you don't like this young lady, I have several others just dying to meet you."

Mrs. Miller was diligent in her matchmaking schemes. When the General Conference sent Harry on a camp-meeting tour that summer, it was a welcome respite from his mother's concerns. It gave Harry the opportunity to speak on his true concern: the needs of China. He spoke on the work being done overseas and made appeals for missions.

But even here he was introduced to eligible young ladies.

"I can't choose just anyone," he confided to his father. "I need a woman willing to be a missionary."

"I understand," his father said. "But you must know that the mission board will not send you back until you find a mate."

In the fall, Harry was sent to the Foreign Mission Seminary in Maryland to do a series of lectures. The assignment was less than innocent, for Harry soon found himself being asked to lecture at the school of nursing across the street.

It was here that Harry met, and soon fell in love with, Marie Iverson. Marie's charming blue eyes sparkled when she looked his way, and Harry felt instantly attracted to her. She carried herself with confidence and dignity, and she found great satisfaction in helping others—a trait that naturally attracted the young missionary suitor.

Marie was quite enthusiastic about Harry's love of his China missions, and when he asked her to marry him she agreed. "But on one condition," she added. "I will marry you only if we take Aunt Bothilde and Percy to China with us."

"Are you sure Aunt Bothilde and Percy want to go?" Harry asked skeptically.

"Oh, yes," Marie said seriously. "She wants to be a missionary too. And she feels it will be a wonderful experience for a ten-year-old like Percy. Oh, please, Harry," she pleaded. "She practically raised me. I feel I owe it to her."

"Well, if Aunt Bothilde wants to be a missionary, who am I to stop her."

Harry's father, who was now president of the Maritime Conference, was asked to perform the wedding ceremony. On Christmas Day, 1907, Harry and Marie were united in marriage. Two months later the newlyweds were on a ship heading to China, with Aunt Bothilde and Percy in tow.

But Harry was disappointed to learn that they would remain in Shanghai, instead of going on to the central China that he loved. The church leaders had decided that the center of the work should be near the Shanghai port and railway. The printing press had already been moved there.

They rented half a building for the printing press from a man named Charlie Soong. Harry and Charlie became great friends, which later helped Harry to establish himself in the medical field. Charlie's three daughters grew up to become three of the most important women in China: Madame H. H. Kung, Madame Sun Yat-sen, and Madame Chiang Kai-shek. Harry could not know then just how much these three women would influence his work in China.

Once the press was fully reestablished, Harry moved their headquarters again. He rented a house near the largest printing press in China. The huge commercial press put out some of the finest books available, and Harry hoped to gain assistance and knowledge from them.

Once again the press was running full scale, and Harry found himself totally devoted to the editorial and printing work. There was simply no time for the dispensary, and his medical work was being severely neglected.

So Arthur Selmon was called on to take over the editorial duties at the press, freeing Harry to concentrate on leading the missions in the China Division and running the dispensary.

But one night Harry was awakened by an alarming cry: *"Fung chung!* The press is on fire!"

Harry threw on his clothes and dashed down the street toward the building, which was already engulfed in flames. Some of his workers had bravely entered the burning building and were tossing books from Harry's library out of the second-story window.

"Get out of there," Harry called to them. "Get out before it is too late!"

"But the books," they called above the roar. "They are so precious."

"Not as precious as your lives," Harry yelled. "You must get out of there now!"

One by one the workers clutched the windowsill and fell to safety. The workers below helped to ease their fall. As the flames leaped higher into the night sky, roaring like thunder, the workers stood silently, their heads bowed low in mournful defeat. One of them clutched a book he had saved from the blaze. Everything they had worked for had been devoured by the flames.

After the fire, the Millers moved into the hill country. They rented a small upstairs apartment for themselves and a lower apartment for Aunt Bothilde and Percy. Setting up a small printing press in a nearby building, they quickly settled in.

Soon a new excitement filled the Miller household: Marie was expecting the birth of their first child. Since Harry found himself away in Shanghai much of the time, just before the baby was due, he moved Marie, Aunt Bothilde, and Percy back to Shanghai. And in November of 1908, Maude May was born.

Chapter 7
A Time of Priorities

The river's muddy waters were swollen by spring rains, and it propelled the houseboat downstream. The boatmen labored to keep the vessel aligned, dodging rocks that lined the shore.

In the cabin, Marie lay unconscious and feverish, in spite of the early April breeze that fluttered through the open porthole. Harry knelt beside her and sponged cool water against her forehead.

The mysterious disease had struck suddenly, and Harry feared that it might also infect the baby. His only choice had been to get his family out of the city and back to the hill country for some fresh air and sunshine. There were so many diseases in Shanghai that Harry had no time to pinpoint a cause.

Poor little Maude cried miserably to be fed, but Marie was too ill to breast-feed the baby. The unseasoned father lifted the tiny infant out of her basket and began to jostle and sing to her, but to no avail.

"Oh, baby," he cooed helplessly. "If only I had a bottle and some milk to feed you!"

But Harry knew that was impossible. The Chinese did not drink milk. Their only source of milk for infants was from breast-feeding.

"Give me the child," a voice beckoned from behind Harry.

He turned to find the boatman's wife reaching out to take the baby. "My baby is sleeping," she said. "I will feed your baby."

Harry knew it was a polite custom for a woman to offer to

feed another's child. In China this was the only other way. But he was also aware that much of the eye disease in China was spread during nursing. The germs entered an infant's eyes as it fed.

"Yes," Harry answered cautiously, "but, please, will you wash first?"

The woman backed away. She didn't wash to nurse her own child.

"Please," Harry explained, not wanting to offend her. "I am a doctor. I know that disease can be spread through nursing. If you will just wash before you nurse, no diseases can spread."

The woman seemed satisfied by Dr. Miller's explanation. Crouching at the edge of the boat, she reached down to catch some river water into her cupped hands. After scrubbing thoroughly, she turned to see if this act satisfied the doctor. Harry surrendered the screaming child, who immediately quieted as she filled her belly and drifted off to sleep.

Harry returned to the cabin and knelt beside his sleeping wife. "What is one to do when a mother is too ill to feed her own child?" he despaired in silence as he stroked Marie's hair. "Or worse, what if she should die? There must be an alternative food for infants."

Harry had once watched a tofu maker grind soybeans in a stone mill and boil the resulting white liquid over an open fire. He then added plaster of paris to harden it. Tofu, or soy cheese, was a common staple of the Chinese diet.

Harry had wondered even then why he could not just drink the milky liquid without the added plaster, but when he tried to drink it, he soon experienced stomachache, gas pains, and diarrhea. Every belch brought up the foul smell and taste of the bitter brew. Still, he could not take his mind off the soybean. Surely there was some way to process it that would make it more palatable for babies. Someday, when he could find the time, he would have to do some tests.

After several weeks in the hill country, Marie was back on her feet, much to Baby Maude's delight, and the family returned to Shanghai.

Harry was appointed leader of the Adventist Church's general missions in China, and in that one year he worked constantly to get the work going. Once again, his medical work was neglected.

A second daughter, Ethel Marie, was born in 1910, and shortly afterward the General Conference sent a full-time superintendent to take over Harry's leadership duties.

"We have another job for you," the Conference informed him. "How would you like to start the first church school in China?"

"I would be honored," Harry exclaimed.

Harry, Marie, and their two baby girls traveled first by train, then by oxcart, to Chouchiakou. The fledgling school began in the autumn of 1910 and quickly gained forty students ranging in age from five to sixty.

A few months after the school was founded, Harry was stricken with the same disease that had taken his first wife away from him. It was a constant battle just to hold food down, and Harry found himself growing thinner and weaker each day. His small intestine grew inflamed, and his liver began to slowly waste away.

"We're sending you back to America," the mission board wrote after hearing of his plight. "There you can seek proper medical care. You are too valuable to lose."

The Millers sadly said goodbye to their faithful workers, and leaving Aunt Bothilde and Percy in China, they boarded a ship to America. It was a miserable trip for Harry. He lay in his bunk, holding his precious daughters, afraid that death would steal him away from them. How he wanted to watch his babies grow!

Harry was taken to the St. Helena Sanitarium in Napa Valley, California. He had lost seventy pounds, and there seemed to be no prospect of recovery.

"I'm sorry," the doctor told him after weeks of testing. "Our experts agree there is no known cure for whatever ails you. There is nothing more we can do."

So Harry checked out of the hospital and went to his parents' house in New Brunswick, where Marie, Maude, and

Ethel joined him. His mother served plenty of fresh fruits and vegetables, and before long it became clear that Harry was actually getting better.

It was learned many years later that Harry's disease was caused by vitamin deficiencies. It is now called sprue and can be corrected with folic acid and vitamin B. But in Harry's day, vitamins were unknown.

The months passed, and finally Harry felt well enough to be Dr. Miller again. He laid plans to start a medical practice in Mount Vernon, Ohio. But first he wanted to visit some of the relatives he had not seen for many years.

Harry's favorite aunt and uncle were Ben and Catherine Honeyman. Uncle Ben was a wealthy farmer who managed many farms and orchards. When Harry was a boy his aunt and uncle had visited on weekends, and because they had no children of their own, they lavished much attention on the growing lad.

"Harry! I'm so happy to see you!" Catherine greeted them at the door. "Oh, Marie, the children are just beautiful." She took Ethel and Maude into her arms and squeezed them tight and then looked seriously at Harry. "I'm afraid Ben is in a terrible way, though. Come. I'll take you to him."

Aunt Catherine led Harry into the parlor, where Uncle Ben lay on a cot, writhing in pain. His clothes were soaked with sweat.

"What happened, Uncle Ben?" Harry asked.

"I took a fall." Ben's face was contorted from the pain. "My hip's mighty sore."

"It's been three days, Harry," Catherine said. "And he seems to be in more pain now than before. Would you take a look at his hip?"

Harry examined the hip. "I'm afraid you've fractured it, Uncle Ben. You really should see your doctor."

"Now, Harry. You know I don't go to doctors. I don't believe in them. I'll be just fine."

"Well, that may be," Harry answered belligerently. "But I'm staying until you're back on your feet. Aunt Catherine, can you put up with us for a while?"

"I'll welcome the company," Catherine exclaimed. She tickled Ethel under the chin. The child shrugged her shoulders and gurgled happily. "You make yourself at home."

Harry bought a hospital bed for Uncle Ben and proceeded to nurse him back to health. Aunt Catherine so enjoyed the laughter of the little ones pattering about that she was in no hurry to have them leave.

"Harry," she confronted him thoughtfully. "Ben isn't yet up to all the work that needs to be done around here. Would you consider staying to help manage the farms? How much money would it take to convince you?"

"It's not a question of charging," Harry answered. "It's just that I must make $3,000 this year to settle my debts. I know I can do that easily if I return to my medical practice."

Aunt Catherine considered the price. It seemed like an awful lot of money, but Uncle Ben felt that it was well worth $3,000 to keep Harry on. Harry agreed to stay for one year.

Seventeen weeks later, Uncle Ben died. Harry took charge of the funeral arrangements, and then he set about planning the crop schedules for the coming season.

All alone now, Aunt Catherine realized she needed Harry more than ever. One night as the two sat beside the fire, Catherine asked him a very difficult question. "If I make out a will leaving all I have to you, would you be willing to stay and care for the farms and me as long as I live?"

Harry pondered the proposition, aware of his responsibilities to his wife and daughters. His bout with sprue had left him weak and unable to care for his family. Managing the farms would provide him with the way to care for them and guarantee a secure future for his children. He talked over his concerns with Marie, who assured him that whatever he decided would be right. Finally he agreed to stay.

Aunt Catherine made out a will leaving everything to her nephew and had it put into a safe-deposit box at the bank. Harry and his family stayed for the first full year, and true to her word, Aunt Catherine paid them $3,000. The Millers were able to pay off all of their debts with money to spare.

Hard work in the sunshine and fresh country air were good for Harry. The homegrown vegetables and farm-fresh produce built him up, and soon he felt stronger than ever. He was no longer satisfied with just managing the farms. He felt capable of doing a much greater work.

"I'm at a loss what to do," he confided to his wife one evening in the privacy of their bedroom. "I'm not a farmer. I'm a physician. My education is being wasted here. Am I really serving God to my fullest by staying here nursing my aunt?"

He paced the floor. "Marie, I enjoyed missionary work. I felt satisfied knowing I was doing the best I could."

Marie stopped him. "Harry, we don't have to stay. Surely we can find something for you to do in the medical field."

Harry battled with his decision. "But Aunt Catherine's will can provide for you and the girls forever."

Marie hugged her husband. "The money doesn't matter," she soothed. "All I need is you."

The Lord ultimately made the decision for Harry when Ben Wilkinson, president of the Columbia Union Conference, offered him a teaching position at Mount Vernon Academy.

"It only pays thirteen dollars a week," he told Marie. "That's not much for a family of four."

"True," Marie said, "but isn't serving the Lord more important than money?"

Harry's father agreed to take a year's leave of absence to manage Aunt Catherine's farms. After that, Harry's brother Clarence took over.

Harry was happy to be well and teaching again, but he longed to return to research and surgery. This was where he felt most needed. A son was born to the Millers that year. Harry Willis, Jr., entered the world in December 1912.

Aunt Catherine lived another ten years. At her death the estate was divided among numerous relatives, but not one penny went to Harry. However, Harry did not grieve the financial loss, for with that loss came the satisfaction that he had chosen his field of service over riches. God would see that his family was cared for.

Chapter 8
What to Do With the Elephant

When Harry accepted the position of medical secretary for the General Conference, he had no idea that there was an ulterior motive. He had been aware that the position carried worldwide responsibilities, but not until he moved his family to Washington, D.C., did the problems of the Washington Sanitarium come to his attention.

Those on the board called the huge gray building the Big Siamese Elephant, comparing it to a white elephant that isn't worth what it costs to keep it. It had taken $100,000 in donated funds to erect the building, and now it was over $168,000 in debt.

Harry lacked the confidence in himself to take on the high position of medical superintendent of the Washington Sanitarium. "I'm afraid," he told the board, "that after ten years away from America, I'm a bit too rusty to do the job justice. Surely you can find someone more qualified."

But the board would not be persuaded. "You are our only hope," they told him. "We will let you take refresher courses at any hospital or medical school of your choosing if you will just accept the position and do your best."

Harry worked long hours trying to keep up with his duties managing the sanitarium, commuting forty miles each day to Baltimore to study, and maintaining his position as medical secretary for the General Conference. In the midst of all this work, a sudden epidemic hit the sanitarium, immobilizing a major part of the staff.

"We believe it may be ptomaine poisoning, evidently from spoiled food," one doctor speculated.

"Yes," Dr. Miller answered thoughtfully. "But it could very well be typhoid fever. Could there be flies contaminating the food?"

"Doctors!" a nurse called as she dashed to their side. "We must find the cause quickly. The superintendent of nurses has just died. We must prevent further losses."

"Take a blood sample from six of the patients," Dr. Miller ordered. "Send them to the Johns Hopkins bacteriological lab for testing. Let's find out what we're fighting."

Five of the samples confirmed typhoid. Harry's correct diagnosis won him the respect of the staff physicians and set a precedent for the sanitarium: Never guess if you can help it. Look past the symptoms to find the true cause of the disease, and then apply the remedy.

Word came from China that Harry's brother Esta had died suddenly while at his post in 1913. The young man had given several faithful years to the China missions. It was a crushing blow, but Harry buried himself in his work and carried on.

One day, a small, pitiful hunchback by the name of Benny Walsh came to the sanitarium in search of help. He had visited well-known surgeons from New York to Virginia seeking relief from an ulcer and other internal complications aggravated by his hunched-over position.

"I'm not sure I can help you," Dr. Miller said after examining Benny, "but if you're that desperate, I will give it my best try." Sending up his prayers to heaven, he prepared to operate.

Benny's hunchback was so bad that he could not lie flat on the operating table, so the nurses propped him into a sitting position as best they could with pillows, and one nurse stood on a stool to hold the ether mask over his face.

Every breath Benny took made his entire abdomen move, forcing Harry to synchronize each move with that of Benny's breathing. It was a difficult task, but Harry found the ulcer and performed a procedure called the Finney pyloroplasty. His patient recovered with little complication.

Benny did not keep his gratitude a secret. He went out and advertised the wonderful job that the Washington Sanitarium had done for him. Soon patients flocked into the sanitarium, including congressmen, senators, ambassadors, and Supreme Court justices. Harry Miller was kept so busy that he stayed on throughout the entire First World War.

In 1915, a fourth child was born to Marie and Harry. They named him Clarence, after Harry's brother.

By the early 1920s, the sanitarium was out of debt and had actually expanded. During the war years, Harry got his start in delicate thyroid surgery. The thyroid is a gland in the neck. A goiter resulted when the thyroid became enlarged, causing the victim's neck to swell and his eyes to bulge. Goiters were quite common in those days, and surgery was very risky. Through his research, Dr. Miller became known worldwide as a goiter surgeon.

Dr. Miller performed twenty-four successful thyroidectomies in a row—an accomplishment that soon came to the attention of the Montgomery County Medical Society of Maryland, and they asked Harry to write a paper on his success. Dr. Miller had hoped to title the paper, "Twenty-five Successful Thyroidectomies," but his twenty-fifth patient suffered complications and died. Still, his record was a great success in those days. The Washington Sanitarium became a thyroid center and continued to grow and prosper.

Continuing his research, Harry learned that aftercare was at least as important as the surgery itself. He developed a form of hydrotherapy that saved many patients who before would have died. As his knowledge grew, his patient mortality rate fell to less than one-half of one percent out of more than 6,000 thyroidectomies! The surgery became less feared, and patients began to seek medical attention in the earlier stages, thus providing an even greater chance at recovery. Surgeons from other medical centers came to learn Harry's technique.

As more and more patients flocked into the sanitarium, the one-time Siamese Elephant now found itself in desperate need of more beds and more space.

"We cannot afford to turn patients down for lack of space,"

Dr. Miller told the General Conference. "Will you consent to building a new surgical unit onto the sanitarium?"

But the General Conference, still shy from the financial disaster of 1912, would not consent. "We're sorry, Dr. Miller. But we just cannot take the risk."

As the space dilemma grew, Harry grew frantic. Finally he decided to take on the project himself. He had blueprints drawn up and excavations made. The building was up and roofed before the General Conference even knew what was happening! And of course the General Conference Committee demanded an explanation.

"Please," Harry appealed, "if you will just let me finish, I promise the building will be fully paid for within one year."

"Based upon the past," the officers commented, "we find this rather hard to believe. But so much has already been done that we have no choice but to allow you to finish. But we warn you, Dr. Miller. Don't ever do this again."

By the time the building was completed a few months later, it was paid for in full. Harry never had to go behind the backs of the board again. From then on, the General Conference listened to his wise suggestions and carried them through.

Many times in his career, Harry would have to take risks, pray for God's blessings, and move forward. He was never too proud to do the little jobs, the dirty jobs. But in everything he did, he gave his very best. Many times his courageous onward march meant the difference in whether the work would grow or stand still.

Chapter 9
Shanghai Surgeon

Marie's eyes glistened with excitement as she carefully folded her husband's shirts and packed them into a suitcase. Young Clarence leaned against the doorpost, watching.

"What's China really like, Mother?" he asked.

"Oh, it's wonderful, Clarence. The culture is so different from America. It will be a good learning experience for you boys. I think you'll find it fascinating. You wait and see."

"But why are we going?"

Marie stopped packing and turned to her youngest. "Because Father and I have been asked to go to Shanghai to promote interest in building a hospital there. Your father cares very deeply for the Chinese people." She hugged him tenderly. "Besides, he can't wait to show you boys China."

"But the girls are staying here." The boy wrinkled his brow. "We will be back for them, won't we?"

Marie chuckled. "Of course we'll be back. It's just a visit. Maude and Ethel need to stay here for school. We've arranged for your sisters to stay in the dormitory at the college."

"OK, Mother. I'll tell Willis to help me pack."

Several weeks later, two wide-eyed boys and two nostalgic parents walked down the ship's plank at the port in Shanghai. It was a time for reminiscing as they walked the busy streets, dodging bicycles and rickshaws. The acrid odor of rotting fish filled their nostrils. Vendors shouted, reminding Willis of a popcorn vendor at a baseball game.

As they traveled up the mighty Yangtze River, Marie

pointed to a small raft that floated by. The boatman's children played happily on its deck, the only yard they had ever known. The Miller boys were fascinated by this strange culture.

The response to the Millers' appeals for funds to establish a new sanitarium in Shanghai was not as good as Harry and Marie would have liked, but Harry grew even more interested in seeing a hospital built here. He envisioned a large, modern facility—one that would stand as an example of the fine medical work being done in America. After a short visit, their task done, the Millers returned to Washington to wait as the wheels began to turn.

In the spring of 1925, nearly three years after the Millers had visited China, a church council meeting was held in Des Moines, Iowa. Dr. Miller was among those in attendance.

"I am sad to report," Elder I. H. Evans announced, "that our efforts to establish a hospital in Shanghai have been largely unsuccessful. If we are to accomplish anything at all, we must have help."

As Harry listened to the appeal, he longed to return to China. Finally he stood to speak. "I have given thirteen years to the Washington Sanitarium. I feel it is well established and no longer needs my attention. My heart is in China, and I would be honored if you would send me back to try to establish a hospital."

"But Dr. Miller," Elder Evans warned, "you must be aware that the illness that almost took your life could very well return. We do not wish to lose such a fine surgeon."

"It has been a long time since I have felt any symptoms of the illness," Dr. Miller argued. "I feel that I am physically capable of taking on the challenge."

"Very well, your request is granted."

The move would not be without sacrifice for the family. It wasn't easy for the children to sell their pony, nor was twelve-year-old Willis too happy about selling the family milk cows, for which he had been largely responsible. Maude was now old enough to enter college the following year and so chose to stay in Washington. Ethel was thrilled that she would get to see her birthplace. She felt she belonged to the foreign land.

With tearful goodbyes, the medical staff at the Washington Sanitarium wished the Millers a safe and happy trip back to China. Harry knew in his heart that the staff he was leaving behind had grown into a fine working team. But he cast any lingering feelings of homesickness aside, and he and his family headed across the sea.

"Have you thought about how we will educate the children?" Marie asked Harry along the way.

"Indeed I have," Harry answered. "I contacted the mission board about starting an academy in Shanghai. He says if we're willing to help found it, we've got the OK."

But progress was slow on the new sanitarium. Blueprints had been drawn up by a qualified architect, and its equipment and staffing needs had been assessed, but only $16,000 had been raised. Much more would be needed.

Harry felt frustrated that he could not serve the needs of the people while he waited, so he bought some medical equipment and set up a clinic in a large rented house. Everyone worked many long hours to refurbish the old building. They turned one room into a small operating room and another into a hydrotherapy department, and they remodeled the kitchen to better serve meals to the patients. At last the building was ready. Now they needed patients.

One day a middle-aged woman walked into the office. "I don't know if you remember me," she said, "but you performed my thyroid surgery back in Washington."

"Ah, yes." Dr. Miller nodded his head. "I remember. So tell me, what brings you to Shanghai?"

"I'm a colporteur now. I have a friend I'd like you to meet." She motioned to her friend. "As you can see, she is in need of the same operation."

Harry gently pushed the woman's head upward to examine her neck. "She sure does. How would you like to be my first patient in my new office?" he asked as he led her into the operating room.

A satisfied customer was Harry's best advertisement, and before long the tiny hospital was as busy as it could afford to be.

Since Dr. Miller was no longer living within the North

American Division, his position as medical secretary of the General Conference had been changed to that of medical secretary of the Far East Territory. In this capacity, Harry traveled to the Philippine Islands to discuss plans for medical work there. While in the Philippines, he was asked to do some goiter surgery and to lecture to the medical students at the college. He was later called back to perform more surgeries, this time to paying customers. Harry used the money he earned to help establish the Shanghai Sanitarium.

A year after returning to Shanghai, a plot of land was selected and plans were laid to build the sanitarium. Everyone was anxious to begin, but try as they might, they could not get the proper local official to put his stamp on the land deeds to legalize the transfer of the property to the church.

China's ambassador to the United States had visited the Washington Sanitarium frequently, and during his years there, Dr. Miller had come to know him well. Now Dr. Miller was called back to America to attend a council, and while there he visited the ambassador in search of assistance.

"The little official expects a handout for his troubles," the ambassador informed him after hearing Harry's story. "There is nothing I can do to change his mind. But I do believe I can help you. I will write a letter to my friend, Mayor Kuo T'ai-chi. He is in charge of the land office and has far more authority than the little official."

A few days later, Harry was on his way back to China to speak with the mayor. Soon the land deeds were issued.

On January 1, 1928, the doors of the new Shanghai Sanitarium were opened. It was a grand facility, complete with surgical and X-ray departments, a laboratory, and a pharmacy. It held fifty beds, most of which were for charity cases or those who could only pay a portion of their bills. A few beds were for wealthy patients. These few would have to support the rest.

One of the first wealthy patients to enter the new sanitarium was the widow of Charlie Soong. Madame Soong was a very influential woman. She had many visitors during her stay, many of whom also began to seek help at the facility.

Without the generous gifts from these satisfied wealthy patients, the sanitarium could not have survived. But Dr. Miller was hesitant to charge the rich. The Chinese preferred to give gifts out of their own generosity, and Harry found that he received a larger gift than the amount he might have charged when he either did not bill them or billed them only a small amount.

While the sanitarium received sizable donations from many well-known dignitaries, perhaps the most surprising gift came from a woman who was brought in following an automobile accident. She had suffered extensive injuries, and her recovery took weeks. While in the hospital, she told her visitors what wonderful care she was receiving and that she was sure Doctor Miller had saved her life. After her release, Mrs. Woo was determined to properly reward the doctor for all he had done.

"Dr. Miller," she proposed one day. "I would like to honor you by having a marble statue made of you to erect on the lawn of the sanitarium."

"I am quite flattered," Dr. Miller answered graciously, "but I'm afraid I could not allow such a statue."

Undaunted, Mrs. Woo searched for a new way to honor the doctor. "Would you allow a bronze bust of yourself to be placed in the sanitarium hall?" she asked.

"I'm afraid I cannot," Harry said.

Mrs. Woo was even more determined to find some way to show her appreciation. Finally she came up with a plan that the doctor could not refuse.

"I will donate $20,000 for the erection of a new dormitory for the nurses—*if* you will agree to have a portrait of yourself placed in the entry and name the new building Miller Hall."

So impressed was she by the work of the missionaries that Mrs. Woo started studying the Bible and was later baptized. The sanitarium became such a success that a campaign was launched to build a large, 200-bed clinic in the poorer section of the city. Donations poured in, and in a matter of months, $200,000 had been raised.

Chapter 10
Feed Those Babies!

Dr. Miller poured the results of his latest experiment into a glass to examine its consistency. He swirled the milky liquid, then brought the glass to his lips for a taste.

"Still too beanlike," he commented, licking his lips. "But it's getting there."

Over the years, Harry had conducted numerous experiments in his efforts to create a digestible milk from the soybean. Thus far, he had managed to cut down on the gas effects somewhat, but there was still much room for improvement. He had yet to devise a means by which to preserve the milk—a very necessary step, since it was unlikely that a fresh daily supply could be made available in China on a large scale. And while his main concern now was to provide for the infants at the sanitarium, his greatest goal was to produce a product that could be distributed anywhere there was a need for an infant formula.

Harry had written to manufacturers around the world for information on homogenization, a process by which the fat particles are broken up to prevent separation. With this new information, he had started his first soy-milk production plant at the sanitarium.

His equipment included a Japanese bean grinder, a Chinese stove for boiling the milk, and an American homogenizer to break down the oil particles in the milk. The resulting milk was so smooth it wouldn't even clog a bottle nipple. But that bean-like taste still lingered in the finished product.

51

Harry poured the remaining milk into the sink. "We'll simply have to keep trying," he said persistently. "The babies are still experiencing too much gas."

He had plenty of infants to test his formula on. It seemed that not a week went by without them finding another abandoned baby on the lawn of the sanitarium. The children's ward came to be known as the Baby Boarding House, and many times Harry was awakened in the night to find yet another abandoned infant. The poor, unable to feed their young ones, slipped them over the wall at night.

One day, a nurse, hearing a whimper in a trash heap, discovered a tiny day-old boy and brought him to Harry.

"I have a gift for you, Dr. Miller," the nurse said as she placed the wailing child in the doctor's arms.

"Well, hello, little fellow," Harry said, cradling the tiny boy. "It sounds as if you are ready for your dinner. Nurse, would you get this youngster a bottle of soy milk?"

Dr. Miller lowered the bottle toward the newborn, who seized the nipple and began to suck in earnest. "I can see there is only one name to call you," Dr. Miller mused. "From now on your name will be Dotsiang—which means soy milk."

Dotsiang lived at the sanitarium for two years until he was adopted by a wealthy Chinese family. During those two years, Dotsiang and other abandoned infants were fed entirely on soy milk, with wonderful results.

Dr. Miller continued his search for ways to improve his new infant formula. On a trip to the Philippines to do surgery, he learned of two new methods: steam distillation and flash pasteurization, both of which would help eliminate the gas and beanlike aftertaste.

Back in Shanghai, Harry and his son Willis, who now worked in the soy-milk plant, tried these two methods.

"I think we've got something here," Harry said as he tasted the first sample to come through the new process.

Willis took the cup and drew it to his lips. "It's the best we've made so far," he said. "That beanlike taste is almost gone."

News of Dr. Miller's soy-milk experiments caught the attention of the media and was published in the *Chinese Medical Journal.* It stated that infants could be nourished from birth as well with soy milk as with cow's milk.

"If it is so successful with infants, why not try it on adults?" Harry wondered. He began using his soy milk on the patients and staff at the sanitarium.

As its fame grew in Shanghai, the soy-milk plant expanded, and Willis became the production manager. Bottle sterilization equipment was installed to provide milk that would keep indefinitely until it was uncapped. Malt and chocolate flavorings were added for variety.

Aboard a ship while traveling to America on furlough, Harry learned of a new method for preserving milk. He noticed that the ship served milk that appeared to taste as fresh on the fifth day at sea as it had on the first. He recalled that on earlier trips the ship had served fresh milk only the first two days, whereupon they were unable to keep it fresh. He asked the cook what made the difference.

"We no longer carry fresh milk aboard," the cook informed him. "We now carry powdered milk. We reconstitute only what we need for the day by adding hot water and butter to the powder. We no longer have to worry about sour milk."

Harry was intrigued by this new method. A spray dryer was quickly added to the soybean plant's equipment for making powdered soy milk to ship to other parts of China. Milk routes were established, and boys were hired to make deliveries. The tiny plant grew and thrived.

Despite Chiang Kai-shek's efforts to restore order, the times were against him. Dr. Miller often received calls from persons in the central government at Nanking seeking medical advice. Whenever he returned from a trip north, he was met by curious patients back in Shanghai wanting information on the nationalists.

Harry was careful not to show a preference for any political following. He was a surgeon, not a politician, and he knew that if he showed any political concerns he could be put out of business. The sanitarium was a sanctuary in the midst of a major political upheaval. Harry needed no enemies.

Chapter 11
Hail to the King

The old topless truck bounced and groaned as it dodged the brush that reached out from either side of the trail. Harry clutched the steering wheel and guided the wheezing monster around potholes and puddles. Harold Shultz and Johann Effenburg, two mission aides, grasped the dashboard to keep from bouncing out of the vehicle. Suddenly the truck came to a stop at the bank of a small creek.

"Grab the planks," Harry ordered with a sigh as he shifted into neutral.

Harold and Johann quickly retrieved two wooden planks from the truck bed and positioned them across the stream.

"Ready!" Harold shouted. "But take it slow."

The gears whined as Harry shifted into first and eased across the planks to the other side. Harold and Johann followed on foot. Each grabbed a plank and threw them back into the truck bed. Jumping into the cab, they reached for a handhold once more. They were on their way to the provinces of Kansu and Chinghai, a vast, sparsely populated region that grew grapes, melons, mangos, and other fruits.

When Harry took over as president of the China Division, not one Adventist lived in the region. However, two colporteurs had been sent to scout the area. Now Harry and his companions were coming to find a place to build a new mission station. The trails were fine for oxcarts and ponies, but they had not been designed for automobiles. With every turn they encountered more obstacles.

When an irrigation ditch blocked their progress, they took shovels and picks they had brought along, leveled the sides, drove the truck across, then rebuilt the ditch. Ropes pulled them over steep terrain and out of muddy bogs and moved boulders from their path. And their two-way radio constantly reminded them that the country they were traveling suffered from the rampages of terrorists.

Often villagers assisted in pulling them out of sand or mud. The people were curious because they had never seen a vehicle in this part of the country. Horses threw their riders when they heard the metal monster coming. But because Harry and his friends were the first to attempt such a feat, they were met with wonder.

For most of a week they traveled, until they reached Lanchow. Harold Shultz was to locate there and later travel on to Tibet. After a good night's rest, Harry and Johann set out again toward Sining, the capital of Chinghai. Mechanical problems plagued them mile after mile, but they were determined to reach their destination.

Just about sunset, the old truck rumbled to a stop on the banks of a small river that was too wide to ford. A ferry boat was tied against the shore to transport oxcarts and people across. Harry and Johann pulled their wooden planks out of the truck to use as ramps and maneuvered the ferry parallel to the riverbank. Just as they had the truck on planks ready to cross, bandits came upon them.

Two of them grabbed the missionaries and held their arms behind them. The others waved guns and knives menacingly and shouted insults at the men. One of the bandits drew his gun to Harry's head.

"Why don't I just kill this one now?" the bandit said, his yellow teeth sneering at Harry.

"Please, take what we have," Johann pleaded. "Just leave us alone."

A sickening laugh filled the air. Harry knew there was no sense in struggling. So instead, he lifted his eyes toward heaven and prayed. "Dear Lord, if I've ever needed You, I need You now. I have confidence that You will protect us."

Suddenly the bandit pulled his gun away. "Get into the truck," he ordered.

They pushed the two men into the truck. The bandits climbed onto the bed and running boards and forced Harry to drive into a tall corral where caravans kept their camels.

"There is no use trying to escape," the bandits jeered as they closed the gate on the pen.

Harry and Johann lay on the truck bed all night, listening to the drunken bandits and wondering what tomorrow would bring. Harry recalled the bandits who had attacked and injured his friend Arthur Selmon and the boatmen on the river long ago. The bandits in the hinterland were not known for their humane treatment either. Usually their victims did not live to tell their story. Harry thought of Marie and the children. Continually he prayed to his Father in heaven.

The next morning, the two men were released without explanation. This was simply not done! As the bewildered missionaries watched the bandits stumble away, they knew without a doubt that God had heard their prayers. The sword of the Lord had triumphed again. They headed across the river and on to Chinghai.

Governor Ma of the local province was so fascinated with the old Dodge that he made the men his personal guests in Sining and helped them find the most suitable location for the new mission. As the truck sputtered out of Sining on its long journey home, Harry was comforted by the knowledge that the gospel would go forth in the provinces of Kansu and Chinghai.

By the mid-1930s, the Seventh-day Adventist Church had a college and mission academies spread across China. One in particular was the China Theological Seminary in Nanking, which had grown from the tiny church school that Marie and Harry had started in Chouchiakou many years before. Besides theological studies, it offered programs in weaving, furniture making, agriculture, food processing, and canning. There were also a bakery and campus kitchen to feed the students.

The idea of teaching vocational skills had never occurred to the Chinese. The wealthy felt that they were above doing manual labor, while among the poorer classes, skills were passed down from generation to generation. If your father was a weaver or a farmer, you were destined to be one too. Thus, no formal vocational training was necessary.

The China Theological Seminary changed that, giving many young people the opportunity to learn a skill that interested them, no matter what their fathers had done before them. It also taught new techniques, making the young people more efficient in their trades.

It was common among the Chinese to worship their dead ancestors, and this custom caused the seminary to hit a snag.

The Ministry of Education issued a decree that stated: "All personnel and students will bow before the image or picture of the beloved founder of the Chinese Republic, Sun Yat-sen, and will recite the guiding principles of the government daily. Failure to comply means disloyalty to the government, and the school will be closed." To make sure the order was fulfilled, government officials visited the schools to teach the philosophy of the late Sun Yat-sen.

If the order had been a matter of patriotism, there would have been no problem. The Adventist Church had nothing against Sun Yat-sen. But to worship a dead man or his image was out of the question, for it would break God's second commandment. The Adventist schools could not obey the order.

The president of the China Theological Seminary, Denton E. Rebok, visited Harry to discuss the problem.

"Dr. Miller, as president of the division, you must do something about this situation," Elder Rebok began. "Our teachers have been threatened with fines or imprisonment if they do not conform to the edict. Word is going around that Seventh-day Adventists are disloyal to the government. Many of the teachers are asking for assignments elsewhere."

Dr. Miller knew they could not afford to close the seminary. Adventist schools were the key to the future of the mission work. The students they taught today were to be the missionaries of tomorrow. These new Chinese Christians would someday replace the foreign missionaries. To close down their schools would be to close an integral part of their ministry.

"I will do everything I can," Harry promised. He knew that later that day he had an appointment to examine H. H. Kung at the hospital. Dr. Kung happened to be the minister of Labor and Industry. Harry thought he might offer some suggestions.

"Dr. Kung," he began, "Seventh-day Adventists are loyal to governments throughout the world. We establish schools and pay for their operation, yet we still pay government taxes just like others who have free schooling for their children.

"In spite of this, the Education Department of Nanking has imposed upon us demands that we as Christians cannot meet. They want to bring in non-Christian teachers, but we are trying to teach spiritual and educational work together. And they want us to bow down to Sun Yat-sen.

"Now we respect Sun Yat-sen very highly as a great leader of this country, just as we respect George Washington in America. But we could never worship Mr. Washington. We cannot and will not meet the requirements of the Education Department, and that means we will have to close our school.

"This would be a loss to China, since we have a new kind of education that China really needs. We provide opportunities for the poor, who would otherwise have no chance for an education. At the China Theological Seminary the students work their own way through school, and they learn a trade so they can be teachers and ministers, and also farmers, carpenters, metal smiths, or government workers. They receive a double training here. We simply cannot afford to close down."

Dr. Kung listened intently to what the respected doctor had to say. After a brief pause, he provided an answer. "I believe in your principles of education very much, and I do understand the situation you are in. However I do not have the power to change the regulations of the Ministry of Education." Dr. Kung rubbed his chin. "But I can offer a suggestion. Why don't you change the name of your school to 'China Industrial Institute' and continue your curriculum just as it is now. You have two phases of your training. It does not matter which one you emphasize in your school's name.

"You will not have to change what you are doing one bit. But in changing the name, you put the institute under my department of Labor and Industry, and you won't have to worry about bowing down to the picture of Sun Yat-sen."

Harry returned triumphantly and told Elder Rebok the plan. Before the sun went down that day, the necessary papers had been signed to change the name from Theological Seminary to Industrial Institute.

A few days later, an official from the Ministry of Education visited the institute, unaware of the agreement with Dr. Kung. Elder Rebok met him courteously, but the official brushed him aside and proceeded. "I am here to see whether you will conform to the edict."

"I'm sorry," Elder Rebok replied. "We could not comply."

"Well, then," the official said, "you will have to close today."

"But we have already closed," Elder Rebok replied.

The official looked skeptical. He had seen students and teachers on the grounds as he entered. Even now he could hear the machinery at work.

"You see," Elder Rebok said, "we have many orders for equipment from the industries in China. Besides, we can't just turn away all these students. The Chinese are very precious to us. Many of our students are very poor. So we have closed as an institute of the Ministry of Education and reopened as the China Industrial Institute under the Ministry of Labor and Industry."

The official left the institute in a huff, and he never returned.

In the following weeks all of the Adventist schools in China changed their names. None of them had to change a single part of their program, and none of them had to close. It was a freedom to be cherished, and they guarded it for themselves as well as for others.

The China Division was careful not to tangle with political affairs, and when Generalissimo Chiang Kai-shek offered $300,000 to begin a fine school, they refused, for to accept would have meant combining church and state, and the government could have forced the school to comply with all of its regulations.

Chapter 12
The Young Marshal

Marie Miller and Mrs. John Oss stood in the foyer of the imperial mansion, nervously awaiting permission to see Marshal Chang Hsüeh-liang, ruler of Manchuria. They hoped that the young marshal could provide them with a list of influential people who might contribute funds for a new hospital. But now that they were inside, they wondered if they were doing the right thing.

Just as Mrs. Oss was about to suggest they come another time, a bodyguard entered the room.

"Your permission has been granted," he said in an authoritative voice. "Follow me, please."

The two women swallowed hard and bravely went in. Marshal Chang stood to greet them.

"What can I do for you ladies today?" he asked cordially.

They were surprised to find such an influential and powerful man so thin and pale. He was obviously addicted to opium.

"We, er, well, the China Division of the Seventh-day Adventist Church would like to start some medical work here in Manchuria," Marie said. "We are hoping to build a hospital."

"Well, how much money do you need?" the marshal asked.

The two women glanced at each other. "We were hoping to collect $30,000."

"Nonsense," Marshal Chang waved his hand in the air. "You cannot build a hospital with only $30,000. Manchuria is too big. We would need a much larger facility to meet the needs of the people here."

The women bowed their heads in defeat, prepared to leave with no funds and no names. Surely they would get nowhere today. But the young marshal continued.

"There is no need to solicit any further. I will give you $100,000 to start."

"That is wonderful," Marie stuttered, still a bit confused and uncertain what she should do next. "But we must speak with our leaders in Shanghai before we can accept such a gracious gift."

"Who must you confer with?" the marshal asked.

"With my husband, Dr. Harry Miller, as well as others with the China Division."

The young marshal leaned back in his chair and folded his arms across his chest. "You have your husband come and speak with me."

Dr. Miller met with the marshal a few days later. "I cannot thank you enough for your generous offer," Harry said as he bowed to the dignitary. "We have wanted to start a hospital here for a long time. Funds are always our greatest obstacle."

"I, too, have wanted to see a hospital here for my people," Marshal Chang confided. "Madame Chiang Kai-shek has told me of the wonderful work the Adventists are doing. I have no problem with furnishing the needed funds, but I do not know how to provide the staff and equipment."

"We are experts in that area," Harry said. "Together we can get this project off the ground."

"I like you, Dr. Miller," the young marshal said. "Not only will I give you $100,000 for a hospital, but I will give you a piece of land to build it on."

Unfortunately, shortly after construction began on the hospital, the Japanese took over Manchuria. The marshal fled with his family to Peking, taking as much of his wealth with him as possible.

The banks in Manchuria immediately froze all funds, and much of the money that the marshal had donated for the hospital project had not yet been withdrawn. Harry went to the bank to see if he could retrieve the funds. With some haggling, the money was released.

The Japanese continued their descent on northern China. A battalion was sent to fight Marshal Chang's army and take over Jehol, an area that Generalissimo Chiang Kai-shek hoped to keep away from them. But the general of Marshal Chang's army felt that even though they outnumbered the small battalion, there was no way to win against the Japanese. He ordered his army to retreat.

The generalissimo was so angered that he flew down to meet with the marshal personally.

"I put you in charge because you command one of the strongest armies," the generalissimo bellowed. "Your performance is failing because of your addiction to opium. I cannot afford to lose Peking to the Japanese while you sit idly by. I must have you replaced."

Marshal Chang brought his family to Shanghai, where he rented a large mansion for himself, his two wives, four children, and forty bodyguards.

Now, more than ever, Marshal Chang knew he must somehow kick the opium habit. He had sought a cure many times without success. So strong was his addiction that he had to have an injection of the drug every twenty minutes to get through the day. It affected everything he did, and it had cost him his command. More than that, his addiction had influenced the addictions of both of his wives. He sent his advisors to speak with Dr. Miller.

"We have heard that you have had success with opium cures and wish for you to come and see if you can help the young marshal."

"I will come," Dr. Miller said after much thought. "But under certain conditions. The wives must also take the cure. It will do no good to cure the marshal if he is still living with those who are using the drug. While treatment is going on, the marshal's general must understand that I have full authority over him and his bodyguards until the cure is completed."

The Shanghai Sanitarium was not prepared to accommodate the marshal's entire entourage of bodyguards, so his mansion in Shanghai was turned into a temporary sanitarium for the treatments. When Dr. Miller found drugs hidden in every conceivable place in the marshal's bed, he promptly had it replaced with a hospital bed. The marshal's physicians had made a handsome profit supplying his opium addiction, and they were in no hurry to see him cured.

"We will start with the marshal," Harry said to his nurses. "Then we will treat the wives. I am concerned about Madame Chang. She has wasted away to only eighty pounds. I hope she is strong enough to endure the treatment."

But Madame Chang feared that her husband would be cured and she would be left an addict, so she insisted that they start with her and Miss Chow immediately. Miss Chow, on the other hand, was not enthusiastic.

The treatment caused the patients a great deal of discomfort, and the withdrawal was excruciating. Knowing this, the doctor kept them under heavy sedation the first few days. But as the days wore on, the withdrawal became more difficult to endure—and the marshal was the noisiest of the three.

Eventually the withdrawal symptoms subsided, and it became easier for Marshal Chang. One evening, as the doctor sat beside his bed, the marshal confided in his friend. "You know, I never wanted to be a general," he admitted. "But my father was a military man, and as is the custom, I was required to follow in his footsteps. I wanted a professional education, but that was not to be."

The marshal hung his head in shame. "When I went into battle and saw people killing other people, it hurt me deeply. These poor victims had committed no crime. Innocent people were losing their lives needlessly, and I was the one in charge. I began to smoke the poppy to escape my turmoil. It relaxed me. My wives joined me, and before long, opium took over my home like a plague."

He turned to face the doctor. "You have taken away the plague and restored my family. I am forever grateful to you, but I know in my heart that it was God who cured me."

Harry's heart thrilled to hear the marshal give credit to God, for he knew that in all he did, God was the guiding force. Because he acknowledged the power of a Higher Being, Dr. Miller felt sure that the marshal's cure would be permanent.

A few days later, Dr. Miller and his nurses prepared to leave the mansion. Marshal Chang paid for their services, but he wanted to do more to show his appreciation. He pressed an envelope into the doctor's hand.

"This is for you," he said. "Go buy yourself a house or an airplane."

When Dr. Miller opened the envelope, he found a check made out to him personally for $50,000! Harry could not accept this gift for himself. "There are some 200 mission workers in China now," he reasoned. "All of them are doing their best to bring healing to the people." His own nurses and staff had given sacrificially, both at the mansion and back at the sanitarium during his absence. He decided to use the gift to build a new sanitarium in Lanchow.

A short time later the marshal donated an additional $20,000 to start a sanitarium in Wuhan, Hankow. Chiang Kai-shek gave $100,000 toward the project, and Madame Chiang Kai-shek had a $20,000 residence built on the grounds so that she could enjoy the treatments at the sanitarium when she was in the area. The marshal was now responsible for the beginning of three new sanitariums.

During the construction of the Wuhan Sanitarium in Hankow, the Communists in western China were working to win the Chinese people over to the Communist party, trying to convince them that the Communist way was superior to the government they had known. At the same time, the Japanese were pushing from the north and the east.

Generalissimo Chiang Kai-shek was caught in the middle, trying to retain a glimpse of the patriotic spirit his nation once held so dear. He divided his troops to fight both the Communists and the Japanese. Fearing the Communists more, he sent Marshal Chang to the northwest area with a greater force to battle the Communist threat to his nation.

But the marshal believed the Japanese to be the greater threat, for they were the ones who had driven him out of his Manchurian territory. He believed that if he put all his efforts into defeating the Japanese, the Chinese and the Communists would work together to eliminate the common foe.

Consequently, his heart was not in his duties, and soon the generalissimo was flying down to find out why he was not conducting a more aggressive attack on the Communists. He threatened to replace the marshal if he did not attack more vigorously.

The marshal became very angry with Chiang Kai-shek, and forgetting his normal common sense, he allowed a small group of officers, who had been influenced by the Communists, to kill five of Kai-shek's generals and kidnap the generalissimo.

News that Chiang Kai-shek had been captured by the marshal spread throughout China. Several generals stood ready to take charge in his absence and suggested that bombers be sent to Sian to overwhelm Marshal Chang.

But the last thing China needed just then was a third war front. Madame Chiang called for Dr. Miller. A special train was arranged to take him to Nanking to talk over the situation.

"Will you come with me?" she asked the doctor. "Try to reason with Marshal Chang and persuade him to release the generalissimo."

"Both the generalissimo and Marshal Chang are dear friends of mine," Harry said hesitantly. "I am in no hurry to take political sides with two friends who have done a great deal for my missionary work. Perhaps you and Marshal Chang's advisors should go without me. If we can just get him to give up his hostage in a friendly manner, perhaps we can avoid prosecution."

Madame Chiang agreed reluctantly. By the time she arrived, Marshal Chang realized he was in a sticky situation, and it didn't take much persuasion to convince him to release Chiang Kai-shek and give himself up. It was agreed that he would be taken to Nanking for a quick trial to save the state's face, and then be released without punishment. In good faith, two planes were called in to fly the entire group into Nanking.

But the marshal was betrayed. The generalissimo quickly resumed his command. Marshal Chang was taken into custody and thrown into prison without a genuine trial. All of his holdings were confiscated by the government, and for decades, he was under protective custody.

In the year that followed Marshal Chang's imprisonment, the Japanese had come as far as Shanghai, and many wealthy Chinese had fled their homeland. Most of the work being performed by the missions was comprised of charity cases, and the hospitals were in desperate need of more money.

Although Marshal Chang's Chinese holdings had been confiscated, he still held large accounts in American banks. Harry visited Marshal Chang's financial advisor. "If the young marshal knew what a great need we have right now," he told the advisor, "he would surely donate the funds to keep the missions going. Is there any way I can get in to see him?"

"There is a way," the advisor answered, "but you will have to be discreet about your purpose. I will give you a letter authorizing the release of the funds for the missions, but you will have to get the marshal's signature on it. When you seek permission to visit with him, do not reveal the purpose of the visit."

Harry decided to take Marie and the boys along to make it look like a social visit, and the guard at the base of the prison mountain issued them a pass.

After a half-hour delay part way up the mountain, while both Dr. Miller and Marshal Chang were interrogated separately as to the purpose of the meeting, the Millers were allowed to go on to the house.

Harry slipped the authorization papers to Marie. "You hold these," he whispered. "The guards will pay more attention to my actions."

Marie later slipped the papers to Miss Elsie Chow, who stayed with the marshal throughout his imprisonment. Miss Chow slipped them to Marshal Chang, and after dinner the papers were again quietly slipped to Marie.

When Harry examined the papers outside the prison walls, he learned that the marshal had authorized another $20,000 for the mission project in Hankow. Even though he was imprisoned, the marshal still carried a deep concern for his people.

Chapter 13
Japanese Invasion

Air-raid sirens, shrill and frightening, filled the city of Wuhan, as the terrorized citizens ran for cover. Dr. Miller and his staff rushed to get the patients in the new sanitarium into the hallways to safety. The bombs thundered ever closer, but at last they faded away.

The fledgling Wuhan Sanitarium was barely finished when the Japanese took over Shanghai on November 9, 1937, and forced the Shanghai Sanitarium to close. The Chinese infantry, with its foot soldiers and ground artillery, had been no match against the sophisticated Japanese army. Japan continued to press north, its hunger for power unquenched by the cities it had already consumed. Harry had no choice but to put the new Wuhan Sanitarium into action before it was ready.

His soy-milk plant was demolished in the takeover, but the Chinese Chamber of Commerce had already offered to finance a new plant in the Philippines. Harry managed to put together a staff from the medical workers who were left jobless in the Shanghai takeover, but funds were desperately needed to stay afloat.

The ambulances worked from dawn to dusk bringing in the wounded after each raid. The Chinese doctors fled the city, until only one remained. The city was filled with chaos.

"We have word that the military school suffered a direct hit," a messenger declared after one of the morning raids. "The casualties are great, but many are still alive."

Dr. Miller and his nurses jumped into the truck and sped

for the school. They arrived to a most gruesome sight. Arms and legs were scattered everywhere. Mangled bodies littered the ground, and the wounded begged to be put out of their misery. The medical team quickly loaded up those they could save and raced back to the sanitarium. Sixteen people survived, but the memory of those they had to leave behind haunted them.

One of the bombs hit a small dispensary that had been set up in the poverty-stricken section of Wuchang. Harry happened upon the scene. As he stood gazing at the heap, he thought he heard a faint cry coming from underneath the pile of debris. Someone was under there. Frantically, he dug into the rubble, tossing huge masses of concrete aside. His hands were gashed and bleeding. The cries were now mingled with a another voice, cheering him on.

He pushed the last chunk of rubble out of the way and peered into the hole. There he saw one of his workers huddled under a table, a baby clutched in his arms. Lime and dust filled their eyes, but except for a few bruises, they were fine.

On October 25, 1938, the last bomb was dropped, and the Japanese took over Hankow. The next morning the Japanese flag of the rising sun flew over the silent city, littered with the bodies of the Chinese.

American hospitals were known to have political immunity during times of war, and now 20,000 frightened and homeless Chinese flocked into the walled compound of the Wuhan Sanitarium. They carried their meager possessions in rickety wheelbarrows and on their backs. They set up crude little shelters, built mud stoves, and settled in to stay. But the food they carried with them would not last long.

Fortunately, the sanitarium had anticipated the need. Earlier the International Red Cross had offered the sanitarium all the rice the workers could haul, and they had filled the entire first floor with 110,000 pounds of rice! Dr. Miller set up a system for distributing the food. The Chinese dubbed him "mayor" of the refugee town.

The camp grew daily as more and more refugees found their way into the sanctuary of the compound. One day a unit of Chinese soldiers entered the makeshift camp.

"We are too tired to fight," they told Harry. "Hankow is crawling with Japanese soldiers looking for any guerrillas still in the area. We have fought our best, but we are outnumbered. We do not wish to die."

"It is not dishonorable to give up after the fight is over," Harry comforted. "I will gather up some civilian clothes for you. You can store your weapons and uniforms in a small building outside."

A few days later a unit of Japanese soldiers came to inspect the sanitarium. To their surprise, Dr. Miller invited them in and treated them to hot drinks, served Japanese style.

"Feel free to look over the compound as much as you like," he offered cordially. "But I would like to confide in you about a certain matter." He led the soldiers to the storage building and told them about the Chinese soldiers who had come seeking refuge. "We have stored their weapons here until you can retrieve them."

The Japanese soldiers were delighted with the collection of weapons and sent a truck that afternoon to retrieve them, keeping a few prized pieces for themselves.

For his honesty, Dr. Miller was awarded a yellow armband, designating him as a neutral party. This gave him the freedom to travel from the Wuchang hospital to the Hankow clinic without fear. Newspapers in Tokyo praised the American doctor who was a friend to the Japanese.

Keeping 20,000 idle Chinese busy was no simple task. Harry assigned jobs to the able-bodied ones. Some became nurses' aides, others clerks, guards, and laborers.

With so many in such close confinement, sanitation was a major concern. Harry's assistant went out time and again to haul tons of gravel and drainage pipe from a business that had been abandoned by its Chinese owner. The pipe was laid out on the grounds and the entire compound spread with a layer of gravel for proper drainage.

One day Japanese soldiers stopped the assistant as he hauled more gravel to the sanitarium. He was taken in for questioning and released with orders not take any more supplies. But by then, several inches of gravel had already been laid.

The "mayor" of the town still had to play the role of doctor to hundreds of outpatients daily. The International Red Cross supplied them with the necessary medications, but they learned that many of the patients were faking illness in order to obtain medicine to sell on the black market. It was immediately ordered that all medicine must be taken on the spot. None would leave the compound. Food was also rationed, as each day Harry watched the mammoth heap of stocked rice dwindle away.

As Japan continued its invasions of China, the war between the two countries grew until it became a part of the Second World War. The entire globe was caught up in a frenzy of fighting. The enormously loyal Nationalist Party considered all foreigners to be a threat to the government and ordered all of them to leave China. Harry and Marie returned to America, but Harry would not be discouraged from helping the Chinese, even from this faraway place. He continued his efforts to help the starving masses among the people he had come to call his own.

Harry's son Willis had been running his own soy-milk plant in New York, and now that the war had forced Harry back to America, father and son got together to make bigger plans.

Chapter 14
Soybean Success

Willis poured a bucket of water into the wheelbarrow as Harry methodically pushed the hoe back and forth, gently blending the liquid with the dry cement.

"Looks just about right," Harry commented, setting the hoe aside. "Let's get those bricks laid." He tossed a trowel to Willis.

Brick by brick, the new 8,000-square-foot production plant was beginning to take shape amidst the fertile fields of the 140-acre farm that Harry and Willis had purchased in Mount Vernon, Ohio. It hadn't mattered that the house on the property was run down. They had outgrown the house in only one season anyway and already needed a larger building for production. They had purchased the land for its seemingly unending supply of clear spring water and its rich, fertile soil—two necessary ingredients for the production of soy milk.

There were other bonuses to this particular location. Its proximity to Mount Vernon Academy provided a steady supply of laborers. And the results of Ohio State University's recent research on varieties of soybeans could benefit them greatly.

Harry had been appointed director of the Mount Vernon Hospital, and most of his salary went to help finance the soy production. During the day he performed delicate surgery with fine instruments, but in the evenings his hands were filled with bricks and trowel.

"I found three used boilers today," Harry told Willis as he slapped a brick into place. "They appear to be in excellent condition, and I can buy them and have them installed for just $3,000."

"That sounds wonderful," Willis responded. "But how will we get $3,000?"

"I'll go to the bank tomorrow. Surely I can get a loan if I use the plant as collateral."

But the loan officer seemed unsympathetic to Harry's plight. "I'm afraid the bank is not interested in taking a risk on a soybean plant, Dr. Miller," the officer replied. "Why not start a dairy farm or a machine shop? Either of these would be far more secure than a soybean plant. If the plant should fail, how would we sell such a novelty?"

After trying unsuccessfully to reason with the officer, Harry decided to ask his brother Clarence for a loan.

"I have no faith in your bean business either," Clarence insisted, pressing a check into Harry's hand. "I will lend you the money, but it's a shame to see you waste your time milking beans when you could be practicing medicine."

Harry had known all along that getting Americans to accept his soy milk would be a challenge. With cows and goats around, why bother to milk a soybean?

"If they will not accept soy milk," Harry reasoned, "let's try producing soy-based meat substitutes for vegetarians—though I do hesitate to call them meat substitutes, since soybeans were used for food long before people began eating meat."

Still, he produced his powdered soy milk, dubbing his new improved version Soyalac. And because America still would not accept his product, between 1939 and 1941 every ounce was shipped to China and the Philippines. However, the bombing of Pearl Harbor brought this exportation to a halt, and soon the war also put the soy-milk plant in the Philippines out of commission.

Cut off from helping the people in the Far East, Harry turned his attention to promoting his soy milk in the United States as a formula for infants allergic to cows' milk. Through testing, he learned that his milk could also help those with diabetes, arthritis, colitis, and other disorders. His new formula for adults was named Soyagen.

Every extra dollar went into new equipment. The factory grew all its own soybeans and sealed its products in tin cans. All was running smoothly until the war forced the government to ban the unnecessary use of tin. Harry's food factory was informed that it would receive no more cans.

"But the factory must have cans to preserve its products," Willis argued, snapping the official notice with his forefinger. "Factories that were canning cows' milk, meat products, and vegetables have not been banned. Why have we been singled out?"

"I don't know," Harry answered. "But I'm going to find out."

Armed with samples of his soy products, Harry traveled to Washington, D.C., to present his case before the committee.

"You will find our products to be quite tasty, gentleman," he began as a tray of meat samples was passed around the table. "Our meat substitutes are very high in protein and just as nutritious as meat in cans."

The committee members exchanged nods as they nibbled on the samples. Harry passed a second tray filled with tiny cups.

"You will find that our soy milk compares favorably in taste to cows' milk, yet it is of particular need to the sensitive diet. To be honest, gentlemen, if everyone used vegetable-based proteins and oils, there would be no need to ration meat, milk, or butter at all."

Harry pulled a chart from his briefcase. "Our statistics prove that animals return only one-eighth of the calories they consume in the form of meat, milk, or eggs. The land used to grow food for these animals could be much more efficiently replaced with soybeans.

"The soybean is the hardiest, most versatile, most nutritious of all foods. It is a miracle food capable of growing in almost any soil. The soybean could very well be the answer to world hunger. We must find alternative methods to meet our growing needs."

The chairman stood to take a vote. "I believe we have all been impressed by your presentation, Dr. Miller. I, for one, agree that you should be allowed all the cans you need. Those in favor, say Aye." The response was unanimous.

Now Harry had to be a salesman, pushing his soy milk at hospitals, asking doctors to just try it on their patients. But the physicians were skeptical. So Harry performed controlled tests on his products to submit to the American Medical Association. He enlisted the help of others to conduct tests on infants, using cows' milk with one group and soy milk with the other. The tests proved worthwhile, for after careful examination, the A.M.A. awarded him a seal of approval.

Now Harry had little trouble convincing physicians to use his products. Still, the milk was being promoted as a formula for infants unable to digest cows' milk. It seemed to Harry that if it could take care of sensitive infants, it could take care of them all. Every baby could thrive on Soyalac.

By now, Harry had sold several of his meat substitutes to a company called Worthington Foods in order to free up more of his time and factory space for milk research. Making money was not his goal, but rather serving mankind in the best way he could.

Dignitaries from around the world came to tour the famous factory. Mount Vernon came to be known as the city with the soybean plant. The bank that had once refused to approve a $3,000 loan now loaned $75,000 for its expansion. Harry's "bean business" had proved successful after all.

One day a fire broke out on the second floor of the factory. The entire upper floor and its equipment were demolished. Harry and his devoted workers were heartsick. But the insurance company assessed the damage and paid them $53,000. Harry used this to add a new steel-sided second floor and update the equipment, which made the factory even more efficient. In the end, the fire proved to be a blessing.

In 1949, at the age of seventy, Harry decided to return to Hong Kong to make arrangements for a new soy-milk factory. The Communists, who had joined forces with the Chinese to fight Japan, had now taken over much of China. Harry was also asked to run the Shanghai Sanitarium once more, for he posed no threat to either the Communists or the Nationalists. His only concern was to see that the hospitals and clinics were secure. The other American doctors had left

China under the advice of the consul general.

But as plans were being laid for the trip, Marie fell suddenly ill, and Harry knew he could not return without his companion. They had worked together for forty years, and he would not abandon her now. Within a few days Marie felt strong enough to travel, and the two boarded a plane for China.

The Communists had taken over Nanking and were moving rapidly toward Shanghai. "Why do you want to go to a war zone?" an airport official questioned as he examined their travel papers. "Nobody is traveling to Shanghai right now."

"We have business there," Harry said. "I am a doctor."

"I wish you luck." The official shook his head. "You're going to need it."

Shanghai was under siege as the plane circled to land.

"Be prepared to jump off quickly," the pilot warned his passengers. "I don't intend to linger."

The plane had barely stopped when Harry and Marie stepped down and dashed toward the terminal. Before the airport officials could reach the plane, it was back in the air heading for Hong Kong.

The two traveled on foot through the embattled city, dodging gunfire along the way, until they reached the sanitarium on the outskirts of town. The hospital had been hit by cannon shells, leaving huge gaping holes in its walls. Between attacks, Harry and Marie moved the equipment to the nearby clinic.

Shanghai fell to the Communists on May 25, 1949. Businessmen fled the city, leaving poorly trained Communists to step in and try to run the abandoned banks and stores.

The Millers were cut off from any contact with the outside world. They moved the equipment back into the sanitarium, made repairs as best they could, and carried on. For several months things ran fairly smoothly, until one day word came that all Americans must be evacuated from China.

Day after day the Millers waited in line for fingerprints, inspections, money exchange, and credit checks. News articles were published announcing the names of those preparing to leave, giving creditors a chance to collect any money due them.

Stacks of documents were necessary to leave China. Those preparing to evacuate stood in one line for hours to have a document approved, only to be told that yet another document was necessary before approval would be granted.

Marie's illness returned, and the constant hours of waiting in line, standing against the elements, took their toll. As much as he wanted to relieve her, Harry was not allowed to be her spokesman. Marie had to stand and speak for herself. At last the papers were complete.

Upon arriving in Hong Kong, Harry and Marie were asked to go to Chungking to assist the hospital and mission headquarters there. The Communists were closing in fast. But when they reached Chungking, the governor warned them not to stay. There was no hope of conquering the Communists. The Millers quickly boarded a plane and flew out of Chungking.

The plane was scheduled to make a stop in Canton, but as they flew over the city, they saw it was already occupied by the Communists, and they could not get permission to land.

Exhausted and saddened by the whole ordeal, the Millers returned to America. But the faces of the defeated Chinese plagued their memories. What would become of the many precious people in China?

Chapter 15
No Time to Retire

Harry dipped a spoon into the warm broth and brought it to Marie's quivering lips. "Just a little more," he coaxed, but Marie felt too feeble for even one more spoonful.

"I'm tired," she muttered hoarsely. "I need to rest."

Harry set the mug on the night stand and pulled the blanket up over her.

"Get some sleep, then," he soothed. "We'll try again later."

He reached for the light switch and tiptoed out of the room. The Shanghai trip had been too much for Marie. The dysentery she had battled over the years had returned in full force, and this time she felt too old and tired to fight it. Harry stayed with her constantly now, tending to her needs.

On October 9, 1950, Marie gave one last sigh and went to sleep. Harry knelt beside her bed and wept softly. At seventy-one, he was all alone again.

Within a year after Marie's death, Harry sold the soybean plant to the Loma Linda Food Company of Arlington, California. Loma Linda actively promoted his products, and soon Soyalac and Soyagen were in demand at pharmacies and groceries across America.

Harry moved to Arlington to assist in food research. He used the proceeds from the sale of the plant to establish the International Nutrition Foundation. Through his research, he developed soy cheese, salad oils, spreads, and ice-cream mixes that contained no animal fats.

The World Health Organization, UNICEF, and the Food

and Agricultural Organization banded together with Harry to establish soy-milk production plants in several highly populated countries, including Indonesia, Manila, and Hong Kong.

In 1953, Ezra Longway, an old friend from his China days, contacted Harry by phone. "How would you feel about starting a sanitarium in Formosa?" Longway ventured. "We know you have the knowledge to do it well."

The very idea seemed ridiculous. "I am seventy-four years old," Harry reasoned. "I should have retired nine years ago."

Ezra laughed jovially. "Harry, you'll never retire. Not as long as you can still walk and talk. Come on, what do you say? We need an expert who knows the language."

The thought of returning to the Far East sent pangs of homesickness through Harry's heart. But he did not wish to return alone. He had taken quite an interest in a certain schoolteacher at Mount Vernon Academy, and now he wasted little time in courtship before proposing. Soon after the wedding, the newlyweds were flying to Hong Kong.

While Harry tended to patients, Mary met with a tutor for language lessons, and one month later they headed on to Taipei, Formosa. Construction on the hospital began immediately and was soon completed.

Ambassadors, foreign dignitaries, the generalissimo, and Madame Chiang Kai-shek were present for the grand opening of the new Taiwan Sanitarium. Many of those present had fled to Formosa from Shanghai during the Communist takeover.

As the crowd quieted, Madame Chiang stood to speak. "This beautiful hospital is about to open for the people of Formosa," she proclaimed. "It cost a large amount of money to construct. You may think the Seventh-day Adventists are very rich to build these hospitals around the world. But I know that the church is not filled with wealthy people. But all of its people give one-tenth of their income. If every person gave one-tenth of his income for such things, what a blessing to humanity it would be."

As the ribbon was cut, the applause was deafening. From its opening, the Taiwan Sanitarium was filled with patients.

Harry had only planned to stay for one year to get the new

facility off the ground. The day-and-night routine was too much for the aging surgeon, and by early 1956, Harry asked to be relieved of his duties. He and Mary wanted to leave quietly to prevent anyone from thinking that the loss of the surgeon would be the downfall of the sanitarium. But friends, patients, and staff would not hear of it. Gifts poured in, until they wondered how they would get everything back to America.

On March 26, a large red envelope was delivered to Harry, requesting his presence at a formal luncheon at the President's mansion. As soon as the guests arrived, Madame Chiang made her grand entrance. "Greetings to all of you," she called cheerfully. "I am so happy you are able to attend. Now if you will all find your seats, we will begin."

The chattering ceased as each guest found his seat. Harry found his place at the very front and turned his attention to the head of the table.

"All rise," a voice called as the generalissimo entered. Offering a handshake to his guests, he asked them to be seated once more.

As the bowls and platters were passed around the table, the chatter resumed until at last everyone had eaten their fill. Chiang Kai-shek stood to address the group, clapping his hands to gain their attention.

"You have all been invited here today to pay homage to a man that we all love and adore—Dr. Harry Miller."

The guests cheered. Harry's mouth fell open. He turned to Mary, whose laughing eyes told him she had known all along.

"We cannot properly reward Dr. Miller for all he has done for our country," the generalissimo continued. "The medical work he has established, the soybean research and the production plants he has given birth to, are a lasting tribute to this great man's efforts. He is a fine Christian, and I am proud to call him brother. In appreciation for all he has done, we wish to award him the highest honor that our country can bestow: the Blue Star of China."

Cameras flashed as the gold medal was pinned to Harry's chest amidst applause and a standing ovation. The story made headlines all across the Far East.

"I wonder if I am really deserving of such a high honor," Harry said bashfully.

"Dr. Miller," Madame Chiang said, bowing in honor, "no one in the history of the Chinese Republic deserves it more."

Ten years later, now eighty-four, Harry returned to the Orient to start a hospital in Hong Kong! Chinese refugees poured into the city by the thousands as the construction crew raced to finish the building, and by the summer of 1964, the 100-bed hospital was serving them.

Throughout his eighties, Harry stepped in to relieve doctors in foreign places until a replacement could be found. He also continued his research in California. He had spent many years perfecting an inexpensive, portable soymilk processor for village tofu makers. Now the Ministry of Health in Japan asked Harry to establish his small machines in all of its 30,000 village tofu factories!

Even in his nineties, Dr. Miller was still in demand by old Chinese families who put their trust only in him. Finally, at the age of ninety-five, he returned for the last time to the United States. But he was not yet retired. He continued his involvement with the Loma Linda Food Company, doing research, lecturing, and traveling to meetings within the U.S.

On Sabbath morning, January 1, 1977, Dr. Miller rose early for his routine three-mile walk, but he returned more tired than usual. He sat down to catch his breath and immediately suffered a massive heart attack. In minutes he was gone.

Dr. Harry Willis Miller's goal was not to attain wealth. He was grateful for the strength to devote so many years to the service of mankind. In his eyes there were no rich or poor, no political rights or wrongs. Only people—all equal in God's sight. Although Dr. Miller sleeps in the grave, his memory lives on—in the hospitals he established, the food products he perfected, and the lives he saved.

Through the years, Harry received many honors and awards. But none of these are as precious as the crown that awaits him in heaven. When Jesus comes in the clouds of glory to bring the doctor home, we know He will say, "Well done, My good and faithful servant."